SQUELCHED
The Suppression of *Murder in the Synagogue*

By T. V. LoCicero

TLC*Media*

Also By T.V. LoCicero

NOVELS
The Obsession (The Truth Beauty Trilogy, Book 1)
The Disappearance (The Truth Beauty Trilogy, Book 2)
The Car Bomb (The *detroit im dyin* Trilogy, Book 1)
Admission of Guilt (The *detroit im dyin* Trilogy, Book 2)
Babytrick (The *detroit im dyin* Trilogy, Book 3)
When A Pretty Woman Smiles
Sicilian Quilt

NON-FICTION BOOKS
Murder in the Synagogue
Squelched: The Suppression of *Murder in the Synagogue*

COLLECTION
Coming Up Short

Praise for *Squelched*

"I sat down and read *Squelched* immediately. It was so absorbing that I could do nothing else until I finished it."—**Rabbi Jack Riemer**

"Although non-fiction, this detailed book reads with the speed of a best-selling fiction novel."—**Israel Drazin**

"...a well-written story of business corrupt attitudes and moral values. The book tells how a top Detroiter and prominent Jewish figure and Republican fund-raiser was able to use his power to pressure the author's publisher Prentice-Hall, Inc., into withdrawing its support for LoCicero's *Murder in the Synagogue*..."—**Elliot B. Halberg**

"That people of Power felt a need to suppress a story that actually reflected WELL on the Detroit community is, in the modern tweeting parlance, "sad." That it could have destroyed a young writer's career is something to consider. That it did not do so is fortunate. I am glad that the author decided, after four decades (!!) to pick up his last manuscript from his professor and finally publish this always interesting tale of deceit and detection."—**Alan Felsen**

"...LoCiccro was contacted by a young Jewish housewife with an amazing story...Thanks to the courage and integrity of this young woman, LoCicero was able to assemble substantial evidence that his book had indeed been suppressed. Only a few thousand copies were ever sold. This is especially sad given the high quality of the book and its sympathetic and positive portrayal of Detroit's Jewish community. Those who arranged to squelch the book actually had nothing to fear from it."—**D. E. Ward**

"Misconduct by a major publishing house? A chain of lies and dodgy maneuvers keep the author's first nonfiction work from ever getting off the ground, despite being well-received by almost everyone who (against the odds) manages to read it? And there is nothing unlikely, bizarre or farfetched about any of it. This conspiracy is as pedestrian as pork and beans, and that in itself makes the story utterly believable."—**Eileen McHenry**

T. V. LoCicero

T.V. LoCicero has been writing both fiction and non-fiction across five decades. He's the author of the true crime books *Murder in the Synagogue* (Prentice-Hall), on the assassination of Rabbi Morris Adler, and *Squelched: The Suppression of Murder in the Synagogue.* His novels include the romance *When A Pretty Woman Smiles,* the coming-of-age literary novel *Sicilian Quilt,* and the crime thrillers *The Car Bomb, Admission of Guilt* and *Babytrick* (The *Detroit im dyin* Trilogy), and *The Obsession* and *The Disappearance* (the first two books in The Truth Beauty Trilogy. Eight of his shorter works are now available as ebooks. They are available as well (along wih several other short pieces) in *Coming Up Short,* a collection of fiction and non-fiction. LoCicero has also published stories and essays in various periodicals, including Commentary, Ms. and The University Review, and in the hard-cover collections *Best Magazine Articles, The Norton Reader* and *The Third Coast.*

SQUELCHED
The Suppression of *Murder in the Synagogue*

By T.V. LoCicero

TLC *Media*

Squelched: The Supression of *Murder in the Synagogue*
by T. V. LoCicero
Copyright 2012 by T. V. LoCicero

For more information on this and other works
by T.V. LoCicero please visit:

www.tvlocicero.com

For Avren Strager

CONTENTS

Author's Note

In the early 1970s I gave my only copy of a recently completed manuscript to Leo McNamara, a former English professor of mine at the University of Michigan. It was a book-length memoir with a rather quirky title: *Joann D'Ark and the Prince of Detroit*. Leo had encouraged me to write it, but then, as sometimes happens in this life, he and I completely lost touch. And so the book was to me effectively lost, a reality that would last for the next three decades. Strange behavior for a writer, you say, simply giving away my last copy of a manuscript that covered in considerable detail the most intense, frustrating and perhaps defining period in my life? I agree, even though most writers I know are pretty strange characters. But I suspect if you read on, you'll come to understand why I needed to give this book away and why I made no concerted effort to recover it for more than 30 years.

In a new Epilogue I've brought the story more or less up to date and explained how *Joann D'Ark and the Prince of Detroit* finally came back to me after more than three decades. In the process, I've tried to give this strange "True Tale" a proper ending.

T. V. LoCicero
April 25, 2012

Joann D'Ark and the Prince Of Detroit

Foreword

What follows is a story I know very well indeed. How I came to know it will emerge soon enough, I trust, along with the reasons why my narrative employs the real names of most of those involved and withholds those of a few others. I have simply set down all the facts in my possession that seem in any way relevant to an understanding of the matter. My effort has been to tell the tale as accurately and dispassionately as possible. The reader, if so disposed, may exercise judgment and draw conclusions.

T. V. LoCicero
May 19, 1972

PART I

Chapter 1

In matching avocado wing chairs—twice recovered and thus reflecting basically conservative instincts—sat L., a 30-year-old writer, and his wife, a home-colored blond with a talent for exaggeration. A high school actress at heart, she rarely missed a chance to embellish the staid reality of suburban life; yet in telling him the most incredible story he'd ever heard from her, she had been throwing away her lines from the beginning.

"Now you can judge for yourself what you think of this story I heard tonight," she had said unemotionally at the door. "I'm not sure what to make of it." Her return had been later than usual that February night from the local community college where she taught an English composition course to assorted housewives, truck drivers, and longhaired teens.

"From whom did you hear what story?" L. had asked as they ensconced themselves in the wing chairs.

"I've been talking for the last hour with Mrs. D'Ark."

He had known then it was about his book, published five months earlier. For the past four or five Thursdays his wife had been telling him how highly one of her students thought of his book and two weeks back had brought home Mrs. D'Ark's copy for him to autograph.

"So what did Mrs. D'Ark have to say tonight?"

"Well, she started out talking about how she'd been trying to decide for a long time whether to tell me something that had been on her mind and preying on her conscience, and how for a while she had been hoping that your book would be a piece of trash so she could forget about it. But then she read it and found out it wasn't

1

trash, and so she felt so ashamed of what *her people* had done, she said, that she had decided she would just have to stick her neck out and tell me about it."

"Yeah, so what did she say, for Christ-sakes?" L. had half-feigned impatience, his expectations low but his curiosity high.

"She said, 'You know what's happened to your husband's book, don't you?' And I said, 'What do you mean?' And she said, 'Well, you know there's been this conspiracy to stop your husband's book.'"

A small knowing smile had turned the corners of L.'s mouth. "And I said, 'What do you mean by that?' And she said, 'I mean there are people who have seen to it that things happened or didn't happen to your husband's book so that people wouldn't buy it and wouldn't read it.'

"So I said, 'Well, we've suspected, and we've heard rumors, you know, that somebody talked to the newspapers in town to keep them from reviewing the book.' At this point I thought she was just talking, just giving me some gossipy kind of stuff that someone else could have made up in the first place.

"But then she said, 'No, no, that's not it, that's nothing, that's chicken feed, that's only a little facet of it. I mean this is a conspiracy that goes all the way to the publisher.'"

"The publisher?" L. shifted awkwardly in his wing chair. "Jesus Christ..." The idea was shocking.

His wife breezed on: "And I said, 'Well, that's absurd, because no publisher is going to cut his own throat. Publishers are dedicated to making money.'

"And she said, 'But don't you understand? There are ways of doing this kind of thing.'

"And I said, 'What do you mean by that, a bribe? Who could do something like that?'

"And she said: 'No, no, you're naive. There wouldn't be any bribe. These people have influence, they're like the Mafia, they have channels, they have connections. And they use these connections to apply pressure, and the publisher thinks, you know, it makes more sense to write the book off as a tax loss and forget about it.' She said she didn't know exactly *how* it was done, just that it was."

"And so you asked her how she knows all this." L.'s smile was gone.

"So, of course, I asked her how she knows all this. And she said she had been at this gathering..."

"What kind of gathering?" asked L. abruptly.

"I don't know. I asked her what kind, but she said she couldn't tell me that."

"How old is this woman?"

"About our age."

"And she has kids?"

"Yeah, two little ones, preschool."

"Okay, so she was at this gathering..."

"Yeah, and the subject of the book came up..."

"When was this gathering?" L. interrupted again.

"I think she said back in October."

"Okay, so the book had just come out. Go ahead."

"So the subject of the book came up, and this man announced to the group that he had made sure that the book wouldn't go anywhere."

"That's what he said, that it 'wouldn't go anywhere'?"

"I guess so. I don't know. Anyway, the people there asked him what he meant, and he said that the publisher had assured him that they would arrange it, meaning, I guess, that they would make sure that the book would not be a big seller, get a lot of publicity, and have a lot of people talking about it."

"And how were they going to do this?"

"Well, she said that the man said that they had raised the price of the book too high..."

"But that would mean," said L., "that this was done, that the approach was made, a long time ago—before the book was even printed. At least before the jacket was printed."

"I don't know," said his wife.

"No, of course it means that." L. felt suddenly short-tempered. "So, go ahead. What else did they do?"

"According to this man, they cancelled the big advertising plans they had for the book."

"He said they had big advertising plans?" L. was skeptical. He had known of the raise in price but had not heard of plans for extensive advertising.

"I guess so. She seemed very positive about that. She said, 'Oh, didn't you know? They had big ideas for advertising this book.'"

3

"Well, anyway, what else? Anything else?"

"Yeah, he said he had made sure that the important reviewers in New York wouldn't review the book."

L. frowned darkly. "How could somebody fix something like that?"

"I'm sure I have no idea. But that's what she said."

L. gazed at their living room walls covered with watercolor scenes of New York City painted by his wife's aunt back in the early thirties. They were fine paintings, and they had not seen light for decades, stuffed in a battered portfolio and lodged for much of the time along with an un-restored 1929 Studebaker in his mother-in-law's incredibly cluttered garage. He found himself fascinated, amused, even, it would be fair to say, elated by what he had just heard.

"I assume, since you haven't told me, that she didn't tell you who this man is."

"No, but she said she was fully prepared to go all the way and tell everything if necessary. But first she wanted to try to get this man to undo what he's done and to get the book some attention. She said if she found that she couldn't do that, then she would tell us everything except where this gathering was and the names of the other people who were there.

"She said she had wanted to do this all on her own without coming to you, but her father and her husband had told her that she shouldn't do anything unless she had talked to you and gotten your approval, that she shouldn't meddle in other people's business without their knowledge, and in any case that she had no right to involve other people, innocent people at this gathering, in her act of conscience. She said she really wants to get her father on her side, because her father has known this man a long time and would know how to deal with him more effectively."

"So what did you say? How did you leave it?"

"Well, I said, 'Look, I don't know what my husband's going to say about all this. Why don't you let me go home and tell him about this first, and I'll have him call you tomorrow?' I thought that way you could get to talk to her and meet her and decide for yourself what you wanted to do. I mean I didn't know what to think of all this. I thought maybe she was crazy."

"Is she? I mean you've seen her every week for the past month or two. Does she seem to be crazy?"

"No, she doesn't. But when she started telling me this story, I couldn't tell. It was just so incredible." After a moment L.'s wife smiled for the first time since arriving home. "You know what else is incredible?"

"What?" He had enough to think about already.

"Do you remember how hard I tried to get out of teaching this class on Thursday nights, how I pleaded with George to let me have a day class instead? If I hadn't been forced to teach this class and if Mrs. D'Ark hadn't been placed in my section, we would never have heard about any of this. It's just so ironic I can't believe it."

Chapter 2

Right, thought L., add one more irony to the string running back to the beginning of his work on the book and with probably more to come. The one he was thinking about now was that this story had surfaced just at a time when he finally seemed to be coming to terms with the experience of offering his book to the world.

It was his first, and for months he had been in something of a funk, waiting for reviews and reactions to come from quarters where he felt it was reasonable to expect some interest. Occasionally he would find a review (usually offering solid or high praise from an unexpected place) or receive a glowing letter from someone of prominence to whom he had sent a complimentary copy. But in general, reviews had not appeared in the most obvious places and opinion had been slow to accumulate.

The sale of the book had been paltry, and there was apparently little chance that it would reach the wider audience of a paperback edition. But, of course, this was an old and familiar story. Every year many excellent new books never got the attention they deserved and were never heard from again. And knowing this, he had not allowed his expectations to become extravagant. One couldn't drop a first book by an unknown author into a market glutted with 30,000 competitors and expect very much. Especially when one's publisher had verified all of those horror stories of stupidity and bureaucratic incompetence in the publishing business. And especially in a year when the American reading taste had run from *Love Story* to *The Sensuous Woman*.

He had told himself these things more than once, and yet he was left with a sense that he had failed to convince more than a few that the story he had spent years assembling held any particular value. It was a little like a dream, he had told friends, in which you suddenly find yourself on a stage in front of a large audience. And so you whip off your clothes and do this fantastic dance, at least it feels fantastic because you're putting all of yourself into it. And finally you finish, and you look up at this great audience—and nothing is happening. Maybe three or four people are clapping in different parts of the hall, but the rest of them are sleeping or playing cards or listening to transistor radios or talking about the weather.

For some time he had not been able to settle into new work. It was a matter of confidence, he knew, and a zest for the infinitely tricky business of putting words together, and he had continued to find it difficult to muster sufficient amounts of either. Recently, however, he had pulled out his collection of short fiction and had begun to polish and expand it.

Apparently his tender ego had finally begun to realize that it had been offered sufficient praise.

For example, he had recently received a letter from Robert Coles, a psychiatrist and author who would soon make the cover of Time as the "most influential" member of his profession in the country. L. had sent him a copy of the book, and Coles had written:

"I was absolutely enthralled by it. It's one of those non-fiction novels that one simply cannot put down. And you did just the right job, maintained just the right tone. I mean, you do justice to the ambiguity of things, and to the mystery of the human mind."

In some ways his book resembled a number of the big sellers of recent years, a heavily detailed non-fiction account of a bizarre and sensational crime. There were important differences: for example, unlike Capote and despite the comment from Coles, he had not set out to raise Journalism to the Novel. But the crime he had researched and written about had offered no lack of strange and appalling drama.

On Lincoln's Birthday, 1966, in the Detroit suburb of Southfield, a charismatic social-action rabbi named Morris Adler had been murdered during Sabbath services in the sanctuary of his five million dollar synagogue. The rabbi had been a man of considerable reputation, and the news of his murder had sent shock tremors beyond metropolitan Detroit to numerous communities across the U.S. and abroad.

Rabbi Adler had also been a man of some controversy in his role as the leader of Congregation Shaarey Zedek, whose large membership included many of Detroit's most wealthy and influential Jewish families. Various community factions had long held strongly felt opinions about the Conservative congregation, including the popular view that it was one of the most venerable and generous in the country. Yet at the same time a recurrent and severe indictment from some Jewish quarters (particularly the ultra-Orthodox and the alienated young) had charged the congregation and its rabbi with leading the way in Detroit to a betrayal of true Judaic values and to a kind of blasphemous capitulation to American materialism. And in the culminating incident upon which the book focused, the charge had been made once again, this time by the 23-year-old son of a congregation family. Confronting his audience in the synagogue with the gun he would soon use to commit murder and suicide, the young man had said:

> This congregation is a travesty and an abomination. It has made a mockery by its phoniness and hypocrisy of the beauty and spirit of Judaism. It is composed of people who on the whole make me ashamed to say that I'm a Jew. For the most part it is composed of men, women and children who care for nothing except their vain, egotistical selves. With this act I protest a humanly horrifying and hence unacceptable situation.

Now as L. considered his wife's report of Mrs. D'Ark's story, though a few things about it remained unclear, his instincts seemed to recognize the feel of truth. Mrs. D'Ark had said she was not repeating hearsay or rumor: her information had come directly from the man who claimed responsibility. Certainly, he thought he could see why a small group within the congregation might do such a thing. The phrase came quickly: "An almost pathological concern for image." But he was intrigued with the idea of a man who had the where-with-all and the inclination to effectively pressure one of America's largest publishers. Of course he had read Norman Mailer on the subject of power and influence in America, and yet he was forced to admit that his imagination had failed him utterly this time. In his deepest puzzlement over his publisher's treatment of the book, he had not suspected such a thing.

In any case, precisely because his instincts were pleased, he knew he should be especially skeptical about this woman and her story. If she turned out to be misinformed, ill-intentioned or insane, he could only lose badly by embracing her tale. He would have to remain as wary as possible. Certainly he must sift back carefully through the book's history in an effort to see how all of it related to this new information. Then more specifically, he would have to consider just what the company had done in marketing the book and attempt to find something that would make the idea of its suppression either credible or impossible.

Suppression? Was that a bit strong for what might have happened in this case? After all, the book had been published, and one could, if one wished, purchase a copy, if only by writing directly to the company. He would have to think about just what to call it. The effort had not been to stop the book completely, but if Mrs. D'Ark's information was correct, there had been a conspiracy to undermine its sale and public discussion. But he didn't much like that terminology either.

Beyond the fact that "conspiracy" had become in America practically synonymous with paranoia, to say that the book's sale and public discussion had been "undermined" would be to assume that they would have been substantially greater without the tampering—in the absurdly haphazard business of book publishing, an assumption difficult to warrant.

No, perhaps all he would want to say if the tale proved true was that an arrangement had been made with the publisher to insure only a limited sale and public discussion of the book. Whatever the case, he knew his foreseeable future would be occupied with an effort to investigate the story and its source, perhaps to verify and in some fashion act on it.

Chapter 3

The book's history had begun with L.'s treatment of the murder and suicide at Shaarey Zedek in an article that appeared a few months after the shooting in the respected Jewish intellectual magazine Commentary. It was his first published piece, and he had just turned 26.

For days after the shooting he had closely followed the stories about it in the city's newspapers, musing and speculating on what seemed to him a bizarre yet significant event. With *In Cold Blood* the sensation of the previous publishing season he was certain that someone had already embarked on a Capote-type treatment. But when almost nothing appeared in national magazines over the next few weeks, he finally sat down and wrote his piece, relying primarily on newspaper accounts and the court record of the young assassin's committal to a mental institution. The editors at Commentary wisely cut most of his speculation on the young man's motives, most of which would be borne out by L.'s subsequent research, but all of which was then premature.

Before the article he had written only fiction—except for some journalism in high school and critical papers in college—and he had first tried to see this material too in fictional terms. But the story seemed inextricable from its pervasive ethnic context, and L., raised in Grosse Pointe as a Catholic and with three of his grandparents from Sicily, felt himself incapable of treating milieu and characterization with the intimate detail demanded by fiction.

He did not think seriously about doing extensive research for a book-length study until a few members of the aggrieved congregation encouraged him to try it. One man in particular, an old friend and colleague of his lawyer father, was especially enthusiastic and offered to arrange an interview with Goldie Adler, the slain rabbi's widow. Reaction to the article was generally flattering, and a few people—one was Dr. Karl Menninger, known as the dean of

American psychiatry—wrote to ask for permission to reprint it in different places, including a hard-cover collection of the best magazine articles of the year. By the time letters from five book publishers arrived, L. had decided the project was a genuine possibility.

About this time L. and his family spent a Sunday afternoon with one of his wife's distant cousins, a middle-aged woman named Margaret, who was working on a long, novelized history of her colorful and eccentric pioneer forebears. While recently living for a time in New York, Margaret had met a literary agent named Jules Fields, who lived in and worked out of the Hotel Wellington on Seventh Avenue, a few blocks from Central Park, and he was now handling her work, which included a children's book and a musical. He hadn't placed anything for her yet, but she was about to leave for New York to see him again, and why didn't L. send her a copy of his article, a brief description of his idea for the book, and a sampling of his short stories, all of which she would urge on Mr. Fields.

He did so and soon heard from New York that Mr. Fields was excited about the book's possibilities; L. should send along copies of the letters he had received from the publishers so that Mr. Fields could more effectively bargain with the large firms he was approaching. L. filled the request, both pleased and somewhat puzzled. Was this the way such things were done?

A man he had never met nor even communicated with directly, and about whom he knew next to nothing, was auctioning L.'s idea for a book to some of America's major publishers.

In fact the first time he heard Mr. Fields' slow-paced, New York voice on the phone a couple of weeks later, he learned that the agent had more or less settled on Prentice-Hall, Inc., one of the country's leading firms, though primarily known for its textbook sales. Two days later on the phone again, Jules Fields announced pleasantly, "I've sold your book."

"What book?" L. asked himself privately and then marveled at the money figure the agent was quoting: "I got you an advance of 8500." A piece L. had seen recently in a writer's magazine mentioned $5000 as the top figure an untried author could hope for.

Along with his wife, L. arrived in New York to sign his contract on the day a young man named Whitman had collected an arsenal in Dallas, shot his wife and mother to death, and then climbed a tower to use anyone who might be strolling below for target practice. Two weeks earlier Richard Speck had annihilated eight nurses in Chicago. Violence in America, especially among its young people, was rapidly becoming one of the most hotly discussed issues in the public forum. L. hoped his book might contribute something helpful to the discussion. Prentice-Hall, Mr. Fields explained, saw it as another *In Cold Blood*.

Years later L. would still rerun certain vivid images and memories of their two-day stay in Gotham City:

- Gladys Carr, the senior editor, a slim, bright, unmarried woman in her thirties, sizing him up over lunch at The Plaza, and finally, with most of L.'s food still on his plate, pulling a long contract from her purse, L. noticing quickly that the due date was seven months away—a three-month extension was provided for, said Miss Carr with tender reassurance—and exclaiming to himself, "But Capote took five years."

- Jules Fields, a short, gray-haired man not far from seventy, heavy, brutal shoulders—in his youth, he said, he had been a blocking back in a semi-professional football circuit in Pennsylvania—and a constantly confidential tone that made the weather report sound like top secret information. With a steady, unhurried pace to his perpetual hustling, he lived alone and worked out of his "private offices" in the hotel drugstore and bar, offering a stream of stories indicating a background in the movie, theatrical, and newspaper businesses, and dropping references to writers (one was Richard Condon) he'd supposedly been connected with in the past: "I never ask my writers to sign anything. A handshake is good enough for me."

- Jules Fields up early each morning stalking his rounds in the proverbial canyons of Manhattan, clearly, and to L.'s dismay, most interested in the movie possibilities of L.'s book. When the time was right he would arrange for L. to go to Hollywood for six weeks on a good salary to work with the scriptwriters. From his experience with professional writers, he said, it should take L. about four months to do the research and two for the writing, after which he'd be willing to kick in a couple hundred dollars, if L. would do the same, to payoff important reviewers who simply wouldn't otherwise deal with the book.

- After lunch at The Plaza and a peck on Miss Carr's cheek, Mr. Fields neatly separating L. from his tougher-minded wife, who went off to shop, and strolling L. into Central Park to talk a little business, explaining that, while he was "strictly a 10 percenter," there were special circumstances in this case. He had been wining and dining editors at places like The Plaza for the past few weeks in the effort to auction L.'s book and in the process had spent at least $500 of his own cash. Now he didn't expect to be reimbursed for the entire amount, after all it was part of the business, but he did think it would be appropriate if L. could supply half of the total he'd spent. L., naive and abysmally ignorant of the ways of this man's world and feeling slightly prosperous because of the contract he'd just signed, finally agreed to a figure of $225, Jules saying as they walked out of the park, "Now that didn't hurt much, did it?"

- Later, L. buying a white gardenia for his wife from a flower lady in the Village, as they whiled away a balmy August evening in streets roamed almost exclusively by fellow tourists and roving bands of 13-year-old gypsies, L. nonetheless feeling that the day had indeed marked an important new beginning.

Chapter 4

Whether its final result would ever be a book with his own words dressed in hard-covers and sold in America's bookstores, or instead perhaps only an interesting but ultimately frustrating experience remained uncertain in L.'s mind even after he had finally completed his first draft some two and a half years later. From the beginning the project had been fraught with obstacles and uncertainties, and for a long time the book as a genuine entity had seemed a vague and fuzzy prospect. He had never even been able to come up with a title he really liked.

During L.'s year in graduate school, some of his short stories had won him a well-known award for student writing, and with a confident step he had left the University of Michigan to marry and take a job teaching English at a small engineering and industrial management college outside Detroit where the duties and demands, he had thought, would be light enough to let him work on his fiction.

The college, however, had turned out to be a less-than-sterling institution, strictly on the make, serving the middle-echelon needs (mediocrity and limited horizons) of the area's giant auto industry, while exploiting its docile students and apathetic faculty.

In his first year, he had been forced to teach more than 25 classroom hours a term, twice the normal load elsewhere, and thereafter matters improved only slightly. His time and energy for writing had been limited, and, with the early arrival of a child, it had taken him three years to save the money he had planned to in one. At the time of the shooting at Congregation Shaarey Zedek in February of 1966, he had been bogged down in the middle of a novel and had decided to quit teaching and devote himself entirely to his writing if only for the six months he had finally managed to pay for. Now he had opted to put aside the novel for a book of non-fiction.

Lately he had chastised Mailer, Capote, and others for abandoning the house of fiction, a sacred place, but he too had felt the gnawing fear that the health of fiction had been somehow impaired by the times, that it had not found ways to deal with the rootless complexity of American life and the new consciousness shaped by the frequently powerful effect of the public realm on the private world. And now that he had come upon a story that seemed to lend itself to such ends, it would continue to pain him that he had not been up to writing it as a novel.

Actually, he had never been fond of either biographies or crime books and took a snobbish view of their literary merits. He had read John Bartlow Martin's *Why Did They Kill?* instead of *In Cold Blood* because Stanley Kauffmann had said it was better, and because after reading several reviews and several pages of Capote's book, he had found himself with no desire to finish it. He thought the Martin book much closer in method and style to the kind of thing he wanted to do, a careful and thorough treatment of the facts that refused to compromise the full complexity of the material for its entertainment value.

He wanted a study that was both serious and readable, but he would not try for novelistic effects on every page, and he would not spend years going back to foggy memories to beg for the brand name of an incidental bottle of pop or the pattern and color of a particular necktie. He felt there would be more important demands on his time. If the story could be told properly, he thought, it might place in focus many of the forces and choices involved in a talented young man's struggle for meaning and identity in the American '60s, tracing a series of conflicts with self, family, friends, ideas and institutions, all culminating in his final, highly rationalized act of violence.

Soon after arriving home from New York, L. had written a note to Jules Fields saying that he seriously doubted his book would be suitable for film adaptation and that in any case he would probably never agree to it.

The task at hand then included a thorough-going history of the 23-year-old slayer, a biographical sketch of his victim, and an integrated description of their milieu. L. embarked with an optimism based largely on a lack of experience and, once involved in a quest for data, soon encountered a variety of hindrances: the traumatized emotions of some of those most deeply involved in the story, which would keep them from speaking of their experience to a stranger; a very live concern with what some saw as a possible invasion of privacy; fear in a few of perhaps appearing culpable in some fashion; and with a few others a claim to knowledge of the "real" significance of the assassination-suicide, making less than desirable a book that might possibly arrive at a different view.

With the aid of Mrs. Adler, who would prove helpful throughout, L. had hoped to secure the cooperation of the family of the young assassin, Richard Wishnetsky, the Adlers and Wishnetskys having been well-acquainted. But he was told the family had been advised against involvement with the book by doctors and others. He had tried other channels and wrote the Wishnetskys a long letter carefully explaining his intention—all to no avail. He couldn't blame them. Under similar circumstances he too would probably have chosen silence.

Chapter 5

The family's silence meant he had lost an important source of information along with access to a number of potentially helpful individuals and documents. But the reputable name of Prentice-Hall helped to open some doors, and L. soon found himself with a burgeoning list of witnesses and sources to track down, reassure about his purpose, and interview at length: a wide assortment of teachers, professors, classmates, roommates, girlfriends, boyhood chums, religious leaders, youth directors, attorneys, judges, doctors, hospital aides, police officials, chance acquaintances, and eye witnesses to the shooting.

To reach some of these people he twice traveled to cities on the East Coast, made numerous overnight visits to cities and towns closer to home and wrote many long, detailed letters to places as far away as Paris, Jerusalem, and Bombay. More often than not he got the information he wanted and eventually would talk to more than 200 people, but for a long time he approached each person on his list feeling that he or she might hold vital information and fearing a rebuff that might scuttle the project. Looking back, he would smile thinly with the realization that though he had spoken with so many, much of his most important data had come from only a handful of people, perhaps as few as a dozen, many of whom, at some point in his dealings with them, had decided not to talk. Only later had they changed their minds.

One who did not was a young man in Boston, interning in psychiatry and described as one of Richard Wishnetsky's most important friends. The fellow grilled L. on his educational background, literary insight, sociological perception and philosophy of life. He then proceeded to a quick summary of the meaning of the assassination-suicide that turned his young, dead friend into a glorified martyr, explaining that L. couldn't possibly write an honest account without "destroying" a great number of people who were guilty of one thing or another in his mind, including the entire membership of Congregation Shaarey Zedek, for whom he expressed a sweeping and bitter contempt. When L. asked, as a ploy and last resort, if he wouldn't care to contribute to their destruction by talking about his dead friend, he said, quite simply, no. And what's more, he explained, L. would get the same negative response from most of those who had been important to Richard.

L. returned home with more concern about his prospects for doing a valid piece of work, but over the next few weeks two important sources changed their minds and decided to cooperate, putting the project back on wheels.

Generally, those he approached in the congregation itself were cordial and helpful. In fact, though he occasionally heard of members who were displeased about his project, he couldn't recall a single instance in which his request for information had been rejected out of what appeared to be a concern for the image of the congregation. The tone was seemingly set by the cooperation of both Mrs. Adler and the man who succeeded her husband at Shaarey Zedek, Rabbi Irwin Groner. One member, a wealthy entrepreneur and former president of the congregation, had been hesitant for a while, but after a reassuring phone call to Rabbi Groner, he spent a helpful 90 minutes with L. in his office on the umpteenth floor of the plush building he owned.

Beyond romancing sources, L. of course faced the traditional challenge of a biographer: the achievement of objective balance when an element of subjectivity is found at every turn—in the opinions, impressions and judgments of a witness, even in the apparently straight-forward rendition of simple facts, or the description of a concrete experience. The inevitably subjective nature of all perception and memory includes, of course, that of the researcher himself, who in recording the data, is forced to assess the character of a witness and the quality of his or her perception, to divine somehow the emotional relationship that existed between witness and subject, to reconcile or make sense of frequently contradictory reports, to search out and dismiss distortion while holding on to what seems to be truth, to assume finally some method of selection whereby a great mass of details becomes a reasonably coherent structure. L. was new to all of this and found in it a surprising fascination.

Almost from the beginning, Richard Wishnetsky's extensive

academic and intellectual activity had seemed significantly related to his personality and behavior. To put it simply, he had been an intellectual. Thus, L. felt he must acquaint or reacquaint himself with a long list of books, plays, and films that had been important to the young man. Also, L. managed to acquire several pieces of Richard's writing including a book-length senior thesis, which necessitated another substantial reading list so that L. might understand and gauge the significance of the young man's rather esoteric area of political science. Also required was a close reading of the books written and edited by Rabbi Adler, which entailed still further research into areas of ethnic and religious studies with which L. had been almost completely unfamiliar.

Finally, because of his felt need to explore in some fashion the major ramifications of the story as seen from a number of different perspectives--sociological, psychological, and especially psychiatric--he soon found himself engaged in a project that plumbed the depth of his own ignorance, confronted him with the unmistakable gaps in his own education and knowledge, and urged him to the impossible task of reading everything that might help him answer the numberless questions piling up in his mind.

Chapter 6

It was nearly a year before he could begin to write, and still ahead were many more interviews to conduct and books and journal articles to study. The deadline in his contract passed quietly as did the three-month extension. On his trips to the east coast, he had explained the situation to Jules Fields and Miss Carr, and they had understood and in fact cheered him on. The contract was revised without a strict due date and Miss Carr explained: "Prentice-Hall doesn't renege on its authors." He was also advised that he had no competition to fear: though at least five major publishers had originally tried to find someone to do the story, the field had been cleared with the announcement of his signing.

The first year had not been easy for his wife. Alone with their 3-year-old son and often without a car, she nursed her own frustrated plans for teaching and writing. After a year, their savings and the paid portion of the advance — $4500 minus 10 percent, minus the $225 subtracted in Central Park — were gone. A teaching position would have to be found for the wife, a day care center for their son.

Writing his first draft took a year and a half. After a year of research he was working with some 75 hours of taped interviews and a stack of notes on long yellow legal paper over a foot high. Yet the project's scope and complexity and the extent its challenge compelled the feeling that he would never know enough to write the book he wanted. Finally, he simply had to give up waiting to learn more, waiting to be whole, good and wise enough to write the book and to just plunge ahead with the hope that all those gaps left by ignorance or blindness would not be serious enough to undermine the value of the whole effort.

Still, uncertainty showed in his exaggerated thoroughness, in his numerous brief essays and descriptions exploring the important areas he felt his story touched on or involved. For example: an historical analysis of the Jewish context, a socio-cultural picture of

Detroit, a socio-psychological sketch of post-war American youth, and a summary of a relatively new psychiatric approach stressing the importance of conceptual thinking in the shaping of personality and behavior. Most of this material he would cut from his final version of the manuscript, but in the initial stages he felt he must set it all down if only to be sure that he understood its significance himself. This, along with his determination to include in his first draft nearly all of the facts he had amassed, caused him to write at each step in the narrative about twice as much as he had thought would be necessary.

The unwieldy length, the limits of fallible informants, his concern about invasion of privacy, the inevitably missed opportunities for dramatic effect and the deep and intimate probing that fiction would have afforded—all these depressed and ground him to a halt occasionally with large misgivings, his forty-nine cent ballpoint useless in his frozen hand.

He had not forgotten, however, the numbing anxiety that had lately plagued his writing of fiction: fear, he thought, that the product of his experience and imagination might, like much of the contemporary fiction he was reading, bear no important relation to what he called reality. The much talked-about crisis of the novel, he suspected, touched on the fact that the form was not often up to a convincing portrayal of the individual's increasingly complex struggle to establish his identity in contemporary society, a portrayal with appeal for a reader very likely involved with identity issues of his own. Thus, the fast-growing appeal of biography, autobiography and first-person journalism, each of which aimed in its way at depicting the true-life quest of a man for his genuine self.

So ultimately he was not unhappy that this story he had chosen to tell was securely rooted in the real in both its public and private dimensions, that it presented a sequence of events about which there was no question of credibility, with motivation to be plumbed by deduction, not produced by imagination.

Despite the occasionally paralyzing doubts, his faith in the story, his day and night obsession with it, always in the end got him moving again. And there were moments when, having added one last piece of information, he finally found a connection or an insight he'd been groping for, when he became too excited to sit at his desk and had to pace the narrow upstairs floor of his writing room in their bungalow, talking to himself as he moved quickly back and forth, working off his exhilaration until he could sit quietly enough to write again.

In January of 1969 he completed his first draft and found that he had written 1000 typescript pages. He had sent the thing off in chunks of 200 or 300 pages to Miss Carr as they were completed, writing all of it in longhand, then rewriting in longhand, then hiring a series of inexpensive typists. In the process he had received only one letter of detailed editorial comment, which had said in effect "Right on" and had offered a few suggestions that had only prompted him to write at even greater length.

Still, he knew the manuscript needed substantial cutting and was not surprised to learn in a letter two months later from Miss Carr's young assistant, Tam Mossman, that considerable work had been done on it. But three weeks later when the new version finally arrived, jammed with a copyeditor's questions on little pink slips pasted to nearly every page, the whole thing apparently ready upon L.'s approval to be sent on to the printer, he was completely stunned at what he found. His original manuscript had been slashed to some 400 pages, and the result looked as if it had been worked over by one of his former students in remedial grammar.

Chapter 7

He read through it as quickly as possible, noting along the way that his portrait of Rabbi Adler had all but disappeared; the seventy page conclusion he'd labored over for two months, containing much of the socio-cultural dimension he had felt so important, was missing entirely.

His letter to Miss Carr began with the line, "Surely this is some kind of strange joke," and continued in a fashion that was rude, bitter, and self-righteous. Later, though, he would insist that its description of the edited manuscript remained accurate:

> What little commentary or interpretation is left is rendered almost farcical by your wholesale cuts. By pulling out a least three-fifths, of the original and butchering the rest you have of course produced an unbelievably inept narrative with frequent passages of flat, insipid, puerile prose (short, choppy sentences and one or two sentence paragraphs with poor diction and no transitions) and an incredible number of falsified or distorted facts, inaccuracies, serious oversimplifications, meaningless or unclear references (to people, places, ideas, groups whose explanation or description has been deleted), definitive statements made on little or no evidence, and mind-boggling non-sequiturs.

In closing, he announced he would edit the manuscript himself, after which they could take it or leave it. From the long, unpleasant letters he exchanged with Miss Carr over the next three weeks, it seemed they were at loggerheads over a basic conception of the book. Prentice-Hall had apparently tried, in a bumbling, inept way, for a quick, slick, commercial product with a chance to pick up big money from a movie deal and the sale of other subsidiary rights.

Toward money L. had the insouciant self-righteous attitude of many in his generation who had been raised in generous upper middle-class homes: he wanted enough to decently feed, clothe and house his family. To want more and to try very hard for it, when millions in the world had considerably less, seemed at least bad form. Even so he was not entirely immune to the appeal of lucre. Money, of course, meant time to write. In fact, he felt, as he wrote to Miss Carr, that Prentice-Hall was underestimating the appeal his book, properly edited, might have in the intellectual, academic, and Jewish communities. He had never seriously entertained the notion that his book was bestseller material or the hope of making much money on it. But he was quite sure there was enough of a market for the book (as he wanted it) to bring the publisher a decent return on its investment.

Miss Carr's assistant, Tam Mossman, would later tell him that for some months she had paid little attention to her work at Prentice-Hall as she lined up an important new position at another firm, and that much of what had happened to the manuscript had resulted from the fact that the editing had been done by a disorganized collection of six or seven people. The too-many-cooks theory, said young Mr. Mossman, was quite relevant here. Every time a section of the manuscript had changed hands the word had been, "It's 1000 pages and has to be cut."

And more often than not when a decision had to be made, it had been to scrap instead of keep. In the end L. took full blame for having left to others a task properly his own.

Full of bravado about how he was going to break his contract if necessary and go to one of the other publishers who had expressed interest in his book, he was in fact not at all sure if this might be easily done, or if Prentice-Hall might be able to sit on his manuscript indefinitely. And this question only intensified all of the old fears, doubts, and uncertainties that came welling up again as he confronted his manuscript once more in an effort to pare it down. He worked through all of May and much of June and stewed with ambivalence at what he was required to do.

Aiming at 700 pages—knowing they would translate to about 400 in a book—he took about a third out of each section as he went. He was pleased often enough, knowing the writing had been improved, the important points emerging more clearly. But there were times when he agonized over the removal of a piece of writing that had cost him something the first time through. He wanted to keep as much as possible but feared that tedium would put his reader off. So, plagued by uncertainty, he stopped at 650 pages, somehow convincing himself that his conclusion wasn't needed after all.

Word that his new version was acceptable came back quickly from Miss Carr. She saw no need for major changes, though Tam Mossman (alone) would go over the manuscript and make suggestions for minor alterations (in lead pencil only). By mid-August, three full years after he had started, L. had gone through the newly edited version, restoring material Mossman had cut (usually paragraphs, only four full pages) or approving his deletions.

Finished, he still felt too close to the book to judge its readability and total effect. He wanted the opinion of others and offered copies of the manuscript to a couple of friends (one he could trust to be pleasant, the other to be brutally frank) and to three members of Congregation Shaarey Zedek: Mrs. Adler, Rabbi Groner, and a professor of sociology who had been one of his most helpful interviewees.

Their verdicts were gratifying. In addition, a couple of them urged him to also include the 25-page epilogue he had finally salvaged from his over-blown conclusion. Sent along to New York, it was quickly incorporated in the final draft. L. at last felt good about his book.

Chapter 8

A production schedule had been laid out and publication set for early in the new year. At the end of October the copyedited version of the manuscript arrived for his approval with considerably fewer pink slips attached this time. Next stop, the printer. At this point, a brief note from Tam Mossman arrived that threatened to blow the whole project out of the water.

The "legal eagles" at Prentice-Hall, said the note, had finally taken a look at the manuscript, and they wanted signed permission statements from all those L. had interviewed and, most importantly, one from Richard Wishnetsky's family.

With deep dismay, L. read a copy of the lawyer's report. The attorney had been asked "to read the manuscript and attempt to suggest certain deletions in order to make the work more acceptable to the Wishnetskys when submitted to them for their consent to publication." Why, he asked Mossman in another of his long and bitter letters, was such a question even put to the lawyer, when L. had explained for the past three years that the Wishnetskys were less than pleased at the prospect of this book and could certainly be expected to withhold their blessing if that would keep it from publication?

"Why ask a lawyer to deal with this extra-legal concern?" he wrote. "Why not a psychologist or for that matter, one of your especially sensitive secretaries?"

And if there was a solid legal reason for asking him to secure signed permissions from each of his interviewees (which he doubted), why in heaven's name was the request only coming now when he had lost touch with many of them and the task would be extremely difficult? As he expected this demand was soon dropped, but the important point was that the Prentice-Hall's attorney had maintained that L.'s book definitely faced the possibility of an invasion of privacy suit from the assassin's family and should therefore not be published without their written permission.

In a long phone conversation with the lawyer in New York, L. decided the man had neither made himself aware of the context of the story—the amount of information about the family already in the public domain—nor thought seriously about its legitimate public interest. The question was, said L., without any signed permissions, exactly what in the book constituted actionable invasion of privacy? To answer, said the attorney, he would have to review the entire manuscript. Having researched the privacy law, L. knew it to be distressingly vague, but he wrote in a subsequent letter to the attorney:

> Of course an assassin is not just any back-alley murderer, but a man who thrusts himself into the glare of the public arena by taking the life of a prominent public figure whose loss shocks, confuses, and saddens the community, which in turn demands its right to know the facts of the crime and the events leading up to it. Armed with the insights of modern psychology and sociology, we know that those events may (probably do) stretch far into the past and involve, among others, familial relationships. As I maintained on the phone, it is impossible to present an in depth view of an assassin and provide the understanding society feels it has a right to ask for, without dealing at some length with those closest to the assassin, including his family.
>
> Compared to the massive "invasion of privacy" suffered by the Oswald, Ray, and Sirhan families in the name of the public's right to know, I think my book does what it has to do in a circumspect and responsible manner.

L. was especially sensitive on this point. At the beginning, in his letter to the Wishnetskys, he had promised to respect their privacy throughout, though their son's final act had made him a public person, legally and morally subject to investigation. In his research L. had avoided approaching other members of the family and had not pressed the issue with people he knew to be very close to them. For a while he had feared that these limits might undermine the validity of the book. But his concern had dissolved slowly as he realized that much of the troubled situation in the home had been outlined in news stories and public court records and that many of its features were classic and predictable. In fact, he had finally included little data on the family beyond what had been made public soon after the tragedy.

He had only rarely been given information too private to use, and in any case, there was no extensive psychoanalytic speculation in the book, which might have involved more personal details. Instead, it concentrated on the young man's experience outside the home and in large measure turned the spotlight away from his family to search the possible effects of his encounters with friends, teachers, books, ideas, institutions, and other social forces. The opinion of those who had so far read the book was that it treated the family with fairness and tact.

While waiting for the attorney's review, L. worked through the copyedited manuscript and saw the early December due date for galleys pass without word. Finally, a few days into the new year, the lawyer's report arrived with a number of suggestions and demands for small deletions. In their first phone conversation the lawyer had told L. that he was not really concerned about *losing* a privacy suit; it was the *possibility* of a suit he wanted to avoid.

Confused by this statement and about the extent of this man's power over the fate of his book, L. finally got some frank explanations from Tam Mossman. It was important, said Mossman, to accommodate the company's attorney, because if he recommended against publication, the firm might decide to protect itself while fulfilling the contract, by making only six books, for example, sending them on to the author, and then calling it quits.

You could understand the company's cautious and conservative approach, said Mossman, only by understanding the facts of its corporate life. Its trade book division, which was handling L.'s book, was a weak sister, financially unimportant and maintained primarily so that the firm could claim to be fully active in all phases of the business. The real money and prestige came to the house through its textbook division and in the legal, medical, technical, and business services it supplied in a series of periodical reports, bulletins, and newsletters.

Thus, whereas other firms might even welcome the possibility of a suit with all its attendant publicity, Prentice-Hall traded on its reputation and could not afford even a hint of scandal or controversy. "The rest of the firm looks upon us as a bunch of wild-eyed radicals," said Mossman.

L. accommodated the legal report as much as possible but argued effectively enough to keep the deletions to a bare and harmless minimum: two short paragraphs, five sentences, and a few odd phrases. Final word of approval didn't come—from the executive editor, said Mossman, a man named Eastman—until the middle of March. It had taken five months to accomplish these few cuts.

Chapter 9

L. had wanted to see his book published early in this first year of the new decade while people were still in a mood to review and assess the turmoil of the '60s in America. At the time the delay seemed gratuitous. Later Mrs. D'Ark would give him another way to view it.

But L. should not be upset, explained Mossman, because Prentice-Hall was highly pleased with the book and saw it as one whose success would not depend on its immediate topicality, but rather on the deeper interest that would bring a steady sale over a number of years.

So the book had been put off another full season and would not appear until October. The galleys arrived in early April, the last half first (naturally) and delayed in the mail, and L. was pressed by the production editor to return them with haste. A notoriously inept proof-reader — he had once been accused of being drunk while proof-reading a graduate English term paper — and by now a bit sick of the whole project, he did something less than the careful job required. Later he would be appalled at the number of typos he found in the finished product.

The remaining $4000 of his advance was finally due, and, though he hadn't heard from Jules Fields in over a year, he knew the check would be sent to his legally established agent. As is customary, the agent's name appeared on the contract, and all payments made to the author were to be channeled through Fields. But L.'s last two letters to Fields had gone unanswered, and so with the man's silence and because L. felt they were incompatible — in all of his troubles with the editorial and legal departments he had never seriously considered asking for Fields' help or advice — he had wondered about severing their connection. Finally, though, he felt that wouldn't be fair, at least until after the agent had received his $400 cut of the remainder of the advance.

Then came a note from Tam Mossman urging L. to formally disconnect himself from Fields, since, Mossman assumed, he was no longer L.'s agent. Prentice-Hall could then send the check directly on to L. Puzzled because he had never mentioned Fields to Mossman, he called the young editor in New York and asked why he had made such an assumption.

Well, because, said Mossman, Fields was more or less out of the business, and Prentice-Hall had experienced some trouble lately in trying to get checks through him to some of their authors. The clear implication was that Jules Fields was less than reliable. This bit of slander soon convinced L. to officially break with the agent by sending the company a formal note to that effect.

Still, he was puzzled. Why, he wondered, had a man so devoted to money passed up $400 to which he was legally entitled? And why had Mossman described him as "more or less out of the business" when L. had learned from his wife's cousin Margaret that Fields was still very much in the business?

Chapter 10

L. used much of his new money to buy a badly needed new car and to take his wife and their son, now six, on their first vacation as a family. Early in July they drove for two weeks in a large circle through the East and Southeast, staying with friends in New Jersey, Virginia, and North Carolina. First up was a visit to Prentice-Hall at their large office complex in Englewood Cliffs, just across the George Washington Bridge from Manhattan.

The company's low-slung buildings were ugly, but Tam Mossman turned out to be tall, lean and good-looking. In his mid-20s, the bright young man of the house had been given his baptism of fire with this book, thought L. Actually, he had come to like Mossman during their long correspondence and was disappointed that the young editor had apparently forgotten the meeting they had arranged by phone the week before.

He already had a luncheon appointment, said Mossman, as did Pat Neger, the young publicity woman L. had requested to see. The three of them talked briefly standing in the reception lounge, and it was decided that though Tam would be tied up for the rest of the day, L. could return in two hours for a briefing from Miss Neger. Yes, the book had come in as scheduled, but Mossman had already put L.'s six copies in the mail to his home address, and there were no more around the office. Miss Neger said she would try to have some brought over by tomorrow from the warehouse in West Nyack.

L. walked across the street to a bowling alley for lunch, amused at his reception: it had been naive and silly, he decided, to expect, if not a champagne party, something more than this.

After a cheeseburger, he found a little park on the cliffs overlooking the Hudson and spent an hour and a half in the hazy sunshine leafing through a catalogue listing his publisher's new fall books. "In a style reminiscent of Capote's *In Cold Blood*..." said the blurb for his book. "Just what I told them not to do," he thought, remembering the advice he had given the publicity department at their request. The catalogue also repeated the mistake in his pen name previously found in the jacket proof. Tomorrow perhaps he would see if it had been corrected. The number of pages listed for his book, 384, was about what he had expected, but the price was a puzzling surprise—$9.95.

A year before, when the book had been first scheduled for publication, it had been listed at $6.95 in a compilation of forthcoming books. Then at the end of the year he was asked to supply the price in filling out a form necessary to secure permission to quote extensively from one of Rabbi Adler's books. Mossman, after a pause that seemed to mean the matter wasn't entirely settled yet, had said, "Say $7.95." So at some point in the last few months, the price had been raised still further. L. winced at the thought of anyone having to pay $10 for his book, but he was determined to believe that Prentice-Hall's bureaucratic foul-ups were behind them now. They must know the market, he told himself.

The title he liked no better than he had when Mossman had first hit him with it just before their editorial battle. Unable to come up with anything he liked enough to fight for and occupied by the hassle over the manuscript, he had lamely acquiesced with the comment that he felt the company's choice, *Murder in the Synagogue*, was derivative and too sensational. It seemed a bit sleazy—appropriate, perhaps, for a drugstore mystery. But then, as he kept repeating to himself, they were supposed to know what sold books.

At two o'clock he went back to the reception lounge at Prentice-Hall to meet with Pat Neger. He had first spoken with her some months before when she had called him to repeat Tam Mossman's earlier request for a copy of the tape recording made by chance of Richard Wishnetsky's indictment of Congregation Shaarey Zedek and the sounds of his fatal gun shots. It was needed, Mossman had said, for a presentation of the book at the semi-annual sales conference: "It will be an electrifying way of getting your work the major sales effort it deserves."

L. didn't think much of the idea but was pleased that Prentice-Hall felt his book deserved a "major sales effort." In any case, as he had told Mossman and repeated to Miss Neger, he didn't have a copy of the tape and saw no chance of getting one. Miss Neger had explained that she would be back in touch with him later with a detailed account of their promotional plans. Now she could brief him in person.

A pretty girl of twenty-five or so, Pat Neger had a neat, efficient manner, short hair, trim figure, impeccable clothes and make-up. B's in English lit at a small eastern school, he thought, though the only personal detail offered was that she liked to go to the beach on Saturdays. She was obviously miffed at Mossman for having failed to warn her of L.'s visit, saying she would try to scrape together some of the details of their plans for his book. What she gave him was a standard spiel, L. imagined, on what the publicity department usually did for each of its books.

Six weeks before the publication date (for his book, October 8) they would send out 300 review copies to all the standard places, preceded two weeks earlier by a letter announcing the book. Also about this time they would mail a single-page news release describing the book and its author to about 500 places, smaller newspapers, magazines and independent reviewers who could then request a copy of the book for review.

As for radio and television, they would first approach the large network shows and, then, if there were any takers, they would try to set up a schedule of appearances on local and regional programs. It didn't pay to try the smaller shows unless the book got some national exposure first, but if it did, then a tour of a few of the better book-buying cities—Pittsburgh was one—would be arranged. Whatever happened, they were definitely planning to do radio and TV in Detroit, said Miss Neger, and they would certainly be in touch with him about that.

L. in fact was not at all sure he wanted to do any radio and TV. The appearance of an author on television often seemed like blatant hucksterism, in which a writer's personality was on display in an effort to spur the sale of his book, while its real content and merits were only superficially touched on, if at all. Yes, occasionally he had seen an interview in which something of substance was actually discussed and a worthy book accurately described. But his own book's complex story seemed unlikely to lend itself to a brief talk show discussion. Still, he'd reserve judgment and, if some offers did come in, decide which, if any, held enough promise to try.

Chapter 11

Before they parted, Pat Neger asked if he could name a few people he thought might write reviews of the book, so that she could send them request copies. L. suggested Joyce Carol Oates, one of the country's most prolific and highly praised authors, who had played a role in his book and often wrote reviews. Also, the editor of the Detroit Jewish News, a widely read and influential weekly serving among others the membership of Congregation Shaarey Zedek. Miss Neger carefully recorded each name and address.

He also mentioned a letter he had passed on to the publicity department, received from a man in Brooklyn who, upon hearing of the book, had scrawled in pencil on several sheets of paper a proposal to write and/or translate reviews to be sent to 300 Jewish and Yiddish publications of which he had a master list. Pat Neger seemed interested and said she would look for the letter. In the meantime, L. could send along a list of about a dozen people who might write reviews or even just talk about the book and thus spread the word. They too would be sent request copies.

What about the list he had already sent at the company's request, he asked, prestigious literary and intellectual names who might be interested in the book?

They would be covered by the advertising department, explained Miss Neger, sent galleys and asked for pre-publication comment. The publicity department usually picked up the list later and sent books to anyone who had not received galleys. The difference between advertising and publicity, she explained, was that advertising had money to buy promotion, and publicity had only books to use in an effort to win "free" promotion through reviews and radio and TV appearances. Subsidiary rights was another separate department which handled the sale of soft-cover reprint, movie, and other rights. She would be in touch with the other departments once the book was launched, but at the moment she was unaware of their plans.

He was pleased enough. Pat Neger seemed capable and reliable, and apparently it was normal practice to send out considerably more books gratis than he would have guessed. If the book failed to make its mark, he thought, it wouldn't be for a failure to get it to enough of the right people.

The next morning six copies of his book were waiting with the receptionist at Prentice-Hall. L. and his little family were excited, the wife and son chanting "Let's see, let's see," and digging hard at the books in a cardboard box. Once in hand, the book looked and felt large and substantial, finally bringing L.'s vague but persistent dreams into sharp concrete detail.

The colors of the jacket were appropriate to its garish title, and on the back his photograph showed a smile that now seemed embarrassed and out of place, not at all the natural and unpretentious grin he had tried for after noting how often a first book presented a photo of its author trying so grimly to look fascinating and profound that he appeared instead dull and pompous. L. had not been critical enough with his own photo, feeling that even the talented photographer and old friend who had taken it could do little more with his self-conscious subject.

His wife didn't help much: "I told you that was an awful picture."

Still, the book seemed well-made, its paper of good quality, the type handsome and large enough to read the forty-line pages without strain. While the colors of the jacket were gaudy, its design exhibited a certain amount of taste, he thought. And the mistake in his pen name had been corrected.

Later in the little park on the Hudson, while their son plunked dimes into the "money binoculars" and tried unsuccessfully to find the Manhattan skyline through its thick smokey haze, L. and his wife read the description on the dust flaps for the first time. Along with the perfunctory superlatives was an emphasis on the young assassin as society's victim, which violated, L. thought, the sense of what he had written. The company's advertising director would soon promise to change it in the next printing.

Chapter 12

Ten days later they were on a small farm rented by one of L.'s close friends (they had taught together at Exploitation Tech) in a lovely valley surrounded by the Blue Ridge, Cowi, and Great Smokey Mountains in the western tip of North Carolina. Alan and his wife Shirley were both fine painters, and their large, intriguing oils filled the rooms of their 100-year-old farmhouse with the exquisite colors of the valley.

Their children, speech lilting with British accents from four years in London, were friendly playmates for L.'s son, who fed chickens, collected eggs, fished and swam in the dark Tuckaseigee River, explored a woods, climbed a small mountain, laughed at an ineffectual old bull trying to mount a disgusted cow and trapped lightning bugs in a jar to make a "living light bulb," all with a kind of basic joy and excitement that L. had not seen in him before.

For L. and his wife there was lots of good talk with their friends, a tour of the college at Cullowhee where Alan taught English, and a trek to an old black homesteader's cabin, abandoned now to a jungle of weeds, with an ancient news sheet that said 1890 tacked to a wall, snakeskin charms still hanging from the rafters, and the litter of lifetimes tossed in a pile from which L. extracted three weathered letters filled mostly with news of illness and death.

They ate vegetables just pulled from Alan's lush garden (a city boy with his doctorate from the University of London, he had learned quickly from his neighbors), sat on a hill behind the house to watch the sun set over the mountains and took long cool walks in the moonlight. The clarity of the night air brought a serenity that L. purchased cheaply from his friends with a copy of his book.

PART II

Chapter 13

"Hello, is Mrs. D'Ark there, please?"

"Uh, she's not feeling well today." The phone carried a young man's voice. A baby was crying in the background.

L. waited a second, then introduced himself. "And I'm calling in connection with the conversation Mrs. D'Ark had with my wife last night after her English class at the community college."

"Oh, yeah." There was recognition and interest in the voice. Probably the husband, L. thought and recalled the guileless, romantic note he'd found on the fly leaf of the book he had autographed for Mrs. D'Ark, an anniversary gift from her husband.

"I would like very much to talk with her about what she told my wife last night. Could you suggest a time when I might try to reach her?"

"Well, I don't know. She woke up not feeling well this morning, and she's sleeping right now. And this afternoon she's supposed to go to the doctor's. Maybe you should try tomorrow."

L. was disappointed. "Sure. I hope it's nothing serious. Maybe I should leave my phone number with you, and when she's feeling better she can give me a call."

The man said that would be okay, and L. hung up feeling this a less-than-auspicious beginning. What kind of illness was this that had struck so quickly and about which he'd been offered no information? Might it mean instability in this woman? The voice on the phone had sounded protective. If it belonged to her husband, might he be less than pleased with his wife's decision to give L. this story?

Three hours later, early in the afternoon, L.'s phone rang.

"This is JoAnn D'Ark." The voice sounded too young, a teenager's perhaps.

"Oh, yes, Mrs. D'Ark. How are you? I hope you're feeling better."

"Oh, I'm all right. I just had trouble sleeping last night. I was up every little while with one thing and another, and this morning I was exhausted. I'm sorry I was sleeping when you called."

"Well, I'm just glad it's nothing serious."

"No, nothing serious. Just one of those nights that happen once in a while. Marv probably made it sound worse than it was. Marv's my husband." The woman's voice, though young-sounding, was composed and matter-of-fact.

"Oh, yes. He mentioned something about you seeing a doctor, and I was a little concerned."

"Well, that's something else. That doesn't have anything to do with this. I have an appointment for a check-up later this afternoon."

"I see. Well, of course, I was very interested in what my wife told me about your conversation last night, and I wanted to go over what you told her in more detail. And also perhaps meet with you, if that can be arranged."

"I'm sure it can. But I think I told your wife just about everything I know about this."

"Yes, well, I just wanted to make sure I got the facts straight. Now this gathering where you heard this man talk about the book occurred in October?"

"Yeah, it was at the High Holidays."

"And was it a large gathering? I mean were there a lot of people there in the room or whatever it was when this man was talking?"

"Yeah, there were a number of people there. I was really just a bystander."

"I see. So he wasn't speaking directly to you. You were just sort of sitting there listening to the conversation."

"That's right."

"And so what exactly did this man say? How did the subject of the book come up?"

"I don't know how the subject came up. Somebody mentioned *Murder in the Synagogue*, and he just said that he had squelched that book, and..."

"Is that the word he used, 'squelched'?"

"Yes. He said he had squelched it."

A terrific word, thought L., amused. Crude and violent. Appropriate.

Asking questions at each step of the way, he led Mrs. D'Ark through the same story he had heard from his wife the night before, though with some elaboration. She was sure, she said, that there had been more than one person involved, that a small group of people at Congregation Shaarey Zedek, especially unhappy at the prospect of the book, had conspired and acted to undermine it. Perhaps one man, the man she had heard talking about the book, a particularly wealthy and powerful member of the congregation, had been asked to approach Prentice-Hall. But from the talk she'd heard from some of the older members in the months preceding the book's appearance and from a few remarks her father had made, she was certain that a small group of men had been responsible and that many more in the congregation had known about it, perhaps even some of those L. had interviewed.

"But how was it actually done?" asked L. finally. "Do you have any idea? Did money change hands? It just seems so incredible that they could reach all the way to the publisher."

"Oh no, you're very naive," said Mrs. D'Ark. "Money wouldn't have to change hands in a case like this. Don't you know the kind of power these people have, the kinds of channels and connections they have? They're like the Mafia. If they want to do something like this, they can do it. For example, and this is just an example: maybe they know somebody who owns the paper mills which sell paper to the publishers, and they can say, 'All right, if you don't do this favor for us, you're not going to be able to get paper.' Or 'The price of your paper is going up.' So the publisher thinks, you know, 'What do I need with this trouble? I'll write the book off as a tax loss and forget about it.' I'm not saying this was how it was done. I don't know how it was done. I just know that it was."

"And the motivation of these people?" asked L. "I assume they were afraid of how the congregation was going to look, even though they didn't know what was in the book or how it treated the congregation. They knew that it would at least rehash the charges that Richard made on the bimah, that the congregation was a collection of hypocrites and materialists and so on, and they figured they didn't need that kind of thing broadcast all over the country. Is that your impression of the way they were thinking?"

"Yeah, I think so. The people I heard talking about it thought you were this outsider, this *goy*—of course they didn't know anything about you—who was trying to come in and capitalize on the situation, to exploit it. And they couldn't see any good reason or purpose for writing this book."

"Right. After all, this crazy kid who shot the rabbi was completely out of his mind so what good is it to write a book about what he said and did. Better just to forget about the whole thing."

"Right. I used to go to the synagogue on Friday nights with my father. My mother died about a year and a half ago, and he and I went every Friday for a year afterward. And I got to know the old men who are about the only ones who come on Friday nights—I was usually the only woman—and I enjoyed them, and I think they liked me too. And I used to hear them talking once in a while about this book that was being written and saying, "They'll never let that book get published.'"

"'They' meaning who?" asked L.

"'They' meaning the big shots in the congregation, the people with the money and the power. You have to understand that for a lot of these people Rabbi Adler's murder was just about the worst thing, the most shocking thing that's ever happened to them. To lose Rabbi Adler, who was like a monument, like something that would never disappear, was bad enough. But to have him taken away from them in the way he was, with the shooting and the accusations and all the publicity and in the synagogue they were so proud of—it was just the most shocking and shameful and embarrassing thing that's ever happened."

"I understand," said L., but only later would it occur to him that perhaps the experience had been so shocking for some that they had been convinced the book would be a highly publicized best-seller even though its author had no reputation and the book had appeared almost five years after the event. And as unlikely as it might seem, perhaps they had envisioned the good name of the congregation impugned coast-to-coast on the Dick Cavett Show.

Chapter 14

L. asked JoAnn D'Ark about her father, and she spoke freely and at length about a man who was clearly important to her. He was, she said, a very successful businessman, running an accounting firm in the city along with a number of other businesses. When L. asked if he might know the man's name, she offered it without hesitation.

"We've always had money," she said bluntly. "And I got to like it a lot myself. I'm very much my father's daughter that way." She had always had a rather intense love-hate relationship with her father, she explained. Actually, as she had told L.'s wife, he was her foster father. She had been adopted as a baby.

"We are both strong-willed people," she said. "Both of us are used to having our own way. But my father, I think, has learned over the years that I can't be cowed or coerced into anything and that when I've made my mind up about something, that's it."

Though indicting amorality in the business world, she admired what she described as her father's shrewd and resourceful adaptation to that world and had, to some extent, patterned herself after him. "I have my father's head for business," she said. "We're two of a kind. We understand each other."

That's why, she explained, her father had known better than to oppose her plan to do something for L.'s book. He had said only that before she did anything, she should contact the author and get his approval, that she not do anything without his knowledge, and that whatever she did, she must take great care not to involve anyone who didn't want to be involved. This was why, she said, she would never be able to tell L. where this gathering was or the names of the people there. She had been trying to get some of them, those who had heard the same thing she had, to come forward with her and confront the man responsible, but she'd had no luck and was quite sure none would be forthcoming.

In any case, she agreed with her father and her husband, whose advice had been the same, that she should not involve these people or anyone else against their will. Her husband, who had formerly worked in management for one of the auto companies and now ran his own firm as a manufacturer's agent, was behind her 100 percent, said Mrs. D'Ark. He too felt that what had been done was terribly wrong and a disgrace to the Jewish community. And for the second time in their conversation, Mrs. D'Ark felt obliged to apologize for what 'her people' had done to L. and his book.

"Well, there's really no reason to feel that way," said L. "From what you say, only a handful of people in the congregation were responsible, and from my experience they in no way reflect the attitude of people in the community or even of many in the congregation."

"I know that, but I just feel that these people are among the leaders in the community and that they should know better. What they've done goes against everything I've ever been taught about my religion and the way Jews are supposed to act. And I love my religion very much; it's very important to me. And I love the Jewish people, but when they do something like this, I wonder, you know, if this is what it takes to survive, then maybe survival isn't worth it. I know I get very emotional on this subject, but I can't help it. I know they probably thought they were doing the right thing, protecting the community and everything, and I know they're not bad people. But what they did was wrong, and they should have known better. Besides there were a lot of other people who knew about this and didn't come forward, and I can't forgive them either. I just think about Rabbi Adler and what a great tribute your book is to him and what he would think about all of this."

Mrs. D'Ark went on to talk about her relationship with Rabbi Adler and how she had become especially close to him during her teen years when she had twice contracted an often-fatal illness. The rabbi had helped to pull her through each time with his emotional strength and spiritual guidance. Later he had married her to Marv, and though she had grown up to see an occasional foible along with the strength and goodness, she still looked back with admiration and gratitude and missed him very much.

Actually, she felt somewhat guilty herself, she said, for not coming to L. right away with her information. The gathering had been in October, but she hadn't received her copy of the book from

Marv until November and then put off reading it for a while. After that she had been uncertain about what to do, though her conscience wouldn't let her alone.

"You have to understand," she said, "that I'm one of those Jews you talked about in the book, who are completely at home in the Jewish community. I just don't know any gentiles. I've had one gentile friend in my whole life. And I didn't know what kind of person you were or how you would react to what I was going to tell you."

Her plans now, she explained, involved a number of things. First, she wanted to write letters, to secure a list of Jewish publications and write to the largest and most influential, describing the book, telling what happened to it and urging that it be reviewed. She had heard from L.'s wife of the book's lack of reviews, advertising and promotion and felt the first order of business was to make the public aware of it. The book, she was sure, had bestseller potential, but first the public had to know it existed and to learn, perhaps from television appearances, that L. was not some kind of ogre out to exploit the community. There was a wealthy man in New York she knew very well, an old friend of the family, who could get him on the Dick Cavett Show. And her father had friends who could arrange an appearance on Lou Gordon's local TV interview show with the biggest audience in Detroit.

Not wanting to dampen enthusiasm L. listened with interest but finally said that he had never seen the book as a bestseller or with the kind of wide appeal necessary for an appearance on the Cavett Show.

"Well, I think you're wrong," said Mrs. D'Ark with what had already become typical bluntness. "I think you underestimate the appeal of your book. I think it has everything. Well, I mean it doesn't have much sex, but it has everything else."

L. laughed and decided not to argue.

She also wanted to write letters to certain well-known Jewish writers who would, of course, have connections and who at least might be able to give some advice. And she thought he should be making appearances before sisterhood and Hadassah groups. "These people have to get to know you as a person," she said, and so she would try to talk to some people, some rabbis in the community, perhaps, and arrange a few invitations. But most importantly she wanted to deal directly with the man responsible in order to get him to see the error of his ways and to reverse the injustice done to L. and his book. She was fully committed, she explained, to the goal of redressing L.'s grievance and was prepared to do whatever was necessary to secure that end. That included telling L. the man's name and, if necessary, making her information public, going to the newspapers with it. But first she wanted to give this man a chance to undo the damage he had done. If he had the power to do something like this, he certainly had the power to undo it.

She would first attempt to appeal to his conscience, to make him see that, probably without thinking about it very much, he had done something wrong, and that he should do whatever was necessary to make amends. She had no great hope for this approach, but if it didn't work, she would explain that if he refused to reverse the injustice, she would give all of her information to the author, including the man's name. That was the reason she did not want to supply L. with the name immediately. She wanted to be able to bargain honestly with it.

"Do you know this man?" asked L. "And does he know you?"

"Oh, sure. I've known him for as long as I can remember. I've known him since I was a little girl. He and my father have been good friends for a long time. Actually, I call him 'Uncle.' I mean, he's not really my uncle, but I call him that. That's the kind of relationship we have. And he certainly knows me well enough to know that I mean what I say, and that I have a very big mouth. Actually, I'm known for having a big mouth. Everybody has always said so. But I can't help it. I say what I think, and I don't like people who don't."

Chapter 15

They talked for a while about what she would ask from this man. Just what would L. like for his book? asked Mrs. D'Ark. L. explained that his primary concern at the moment was getting the book into a paperback edition, to make it available at a reasonable price. And he feared that if pressure had been brought to bear on Prentice-Hall, the company would simply never sell the reprint rights. These people certainly wouldn't want copies of his book on paperback stands around the country. Mrs. D'Ark agreed.

Beyond that, said L., he had hoped the publisher would do a little common-sense advertising to announce the book and briefly indicate reaction to it. Not much, because he didn't really believe in the efficacy of a lot of advertising for this book. But enough to let certain segments of the reading public know that the book was available and had been praised by some highly respected people. And he would like to see some reviews in places where they might be expected, certain newspapers, journals, and magazines.

Mrs. D'Ark thought L. too easily pleased and said she felt he should get some money out of these people and use it to advertise his book in the way it should have been in the first place. No, said L., he wanted no money from them. He wouldn't feel right taking it. It smacked too much of blackmail.

But they had deprived L. of his rightful income, argued Mrs. D'Ark. He had worked for four years and didn't have a penny to show for it. It was an argument L. would get from a few of his friends and occasionally his wife over the next few months. Well, said L., he had received the $8500 advance and that was probably more than what most books brought their authors these days. You couldn't write a serious book and expect to make money on it. It might happen occasionally out of sheer luck, but you couldn't expect it. He simply wouldn't know what to ask for, because he had no idea what if anything the book might have made with a fair chance on the market. Perhaps, there would have been no difference.

This was one reason, said L., that the idea of legal action, even if a strong case could be constructed (which L. doubted), held no appeal for him. Another was that a suit would probably cause an enormous scandal, and he would hate to see that kind of thing break over the Jewish community. The case would probably drag on for years, and there would be a lot of ugly feeling and unpleasantness for everyone involved. There would be a lot of publicity, but all of the wrong kind, and people would get a distorted view of his book.

Well, said Mrs. D'Ark, she and Marv had talked to their lawyer about all of this before she had spoken to L.'s wife, and he had said that even with all of Mrs. D'Ark's information, there was probably little L. could do legally. She was sure, for example, that her story would be contradicted by every person at that gathering. They were all very close to this man and would all stick together, as she had found in trying to recruit support among them for what she was doing.

She would continue her efforts to find someone to stand up with her, but actually, she thought her best chance for success was to get her father on her side—even though there were times when she suspected that he too might have been involved in the plot against the book.

"Do you really think he might have?" asked L.

"I wouldn't put it past him," said Mrs. D'Ark. Nonetheless, she felt they stood a much better chance of succeeding, if her father would agree to help. After all he had known this man very well for years. They had been in business deals together. Her father would know how to deal with him and could get together with others to put more effective pressure on him.

"Could this man hurt your father financially?" asked L.

"No, I don't think so," said Mrs. D'Ark in a tone indicating that this possibility as well as L's next question had already been considered.

"How about your husband's business? Could he hurt that?"

"No, most of Marv's business, maybe 80 percent of it, is done with non-Jews."

Mrs. D'Ark asked about L.'s connections in the Jewish community. Well, he said, of course he was on very good terms with both Mrs. Adler and Rabbi Groner, the current leader of Congregation

Shaarey Zedek. And his father, a labor-relations attorney for 37 years in the city, and his mother, long active in several cultural organizations, had a large number of good friends and acquaintances in the Jewish community, though probably not among that circle of extremely wealthy families that Mrs. D'Ark must be talking about. His father's friends were probably for the most part lawyers and judges.

Unfortunately, said Mrs. D'Ark, only the big-money people would exert influence in this case. She had been thinking about telling the story to Mrs. Adler, whom she knew quite well, but had hesitated, not wanting to thrust this new unpleasantness on a woman who had gone through so much.

"I doubt if she knows anything about this," said L. "I imagine these people would try hard to keep a story like this from both Mrs. Adler and Rabbi Groner." L. had sent a new year's card to each back in early January and had received one in return from Mrs. Adler. Later he had spoken with her briefly on the phone and, putting a good face on it, had told her the book seemed to be doing fairly well in Detroit though he had no figures. She had mentioned friends around the country who had not been able to find the book, and L. had said, yes, that was a problem. He had not heard from Rabbi Groner, though in the past he had received nothing but generous help and good will from the rabbi.

Rabbi Groner wouldn't be able to do anything, anyway, said Mrs. D'Ark. His position was politically sensitive, caught as he was between different factions in the congregation and paid and retained by the very people who were responsible for the fate of L.'s book.

L. said the only other rabbi he'd been in touch with since the book's publication was Rabbi Max Kapustin, the director of the Hillel Center at Wayne State University in Detroit. Rabbi Kapustin, who had known both Richard Wishnetsky and Rabbi Adler, had given him a long and very helpful interview during his research and then a month ago had invited him down to speak to students at the center on a subject related to the book. L. had accepted (it was his only such appearance) and on a Thursday afternoon in the middle of January had traveled down to the Hillel quarters in the new Irwin Cohn Building on the campus at Wayne State. Before reading his paper, he had chatted for a while with the Berlin-educated rabbi, who was very kind in his comments about L.'s book and interested in how it was doing.

Not very well, L. had said, and he had recited some of his complaints over his publisher's treatment of the book. And despite receiving some excellent comments from important people and a number of favorable reviews in places as unlikely as Pomona, California, and Fort Worth, Texas, the book had not been reviewed in Detroit's two major papers. After all, this was one of the most dramatic and important stories in Detroit in the past decade. It just didn't make sense.

"Well, you know," Rabbi Kapustin had said, "somebody may have talked to somebody."

"Well, of course, that's what I finally decided," L. had replied. "I know there were people who were not happy about the book, the Wishnetsky family, for example, and I'm sure someone got to the papers and suggested, you know, it would be better for everyone involved if this book didn't get a lot of play."

Rabbi Kapustin's remark had been L.'s only hint that someone might have acted against the book. Mrs. D'Ark said she had known Rabbi Kapustin for a decade, ever since the year she had attended Wayne State and had spent a lot of time around the Hillel Center, seeing the rabbi nearly every day.

"Oh, yes!" said JoAnn D'Ark. "It was like an oasis. My friends and I had come from schools where the percentage of Jewish kids was very high and here we were at this big university in the midst of all these *goyim*, and sometimes I just couldn't get back to the Hillel house fast enough. I know that may sound terrible to say, but that's the way I felt."

Mrs. D'Ark said she might get in touch with Rabbi Kapustin to see if he knew anything more about the book, and it was mutually agreed that, at least for the time being, it would be better if she and L. didn't know one another, if officially they had not yet spoken together about the book. For one thing, there would be less chance that the man she wanted to confront would learn that she had already told L. her story. For another, it would be better if she appeared to be acting without knowing L., since it might later be said that he had recruited her efforts. This rather fuzzy notion issued from L.'s unspoken desire to keep his distance until he was sure of JoAnn D'Ark. Their conversation had been reassuring, but she was still only a voice on the phone.

With their respective Sabbaths coming up—L. had long ago stopped observing his but would learn that Mrs. D'Ark and her family were serious enough about theirs to not answer the phone—they arranged to meet on Monday. L. would drop by the D'Ark home in a neighboring suburb in the afternoon.

Finally, they talked briefly about JoAnn D'Ark's love for books and her admiration for good writing. L. repeated his wife's report that Mrs. D'Ark was the best writer in her class, potentially a good writer if she worked diligently, a high compliment from a demanding teacher. Mrs. D'Ark, however, disparaged her own efforts and skill and accused L. of trying to please her with false flattery. There was annoyance and disappointment in her voice as she said goodbye, and L. hung up with a sense that it might not always be easy to deal with this woman who had entered his life as an angel but remained for his wife a student.

Chapter 16

On Monday morning when L. called Mrs. D'Ark to confirm their meeting later in the day, her response was quick and good-humored: "Well, did your father get a Dun and Bradstreet rating on my father?"

L. laughed and said no, but, of course, after their talk on Friday he had called his father and had been mildly surprised when her father's name had not registered. L. had long suspected that his father, a warm and gregarious man, knew at least half the residents of Metro Detroit. His father had quickly found the name, however, in a professional directory along with a suburban office address. If necessary the man was a phone call away.

"He has a good one," said Mrs. D'Ark, meaning her father's rating.

"I'm sure he does," said L., confident that his father, while not going to such lengths, would check on the man in his own fashion. Predictably, his father's reaction to Mrs. D'Ark's information about the book had been calm and cautious. He had been only as shocked as one who had traveled in the world of American business for nearly 40 years could be. Watch and listen to this woman carefully, he had counseled, but keep your distance and let her take the initiative.

There had been no hesitation with JoAnn D'Ark. She had already called Rabbi Kapustin, learned that he "knew" about what had been done to L.'s book, and arranged to meet him the next day at the Hillel center. She had not told the rabbi about having spoken with L. or about what she wanted to do. She had simply opened with the line, "Isn't it terrible what so-and-so-did to this book about the murder of Rabbi Adler?" And the rabbi had agreed.

With wrong and missed turns on the way, L. arrived a half-hour late at the D'Ark home, a ranch in a relatively new subdivision. At the door Mrs. D'Ark said, "Yes, I recognize you from the picture on

51

the back of your book."

He shook hands with Marv, the husband looking friendly and inquisitive. Mrs. D'Ark wore a well-tailored black pantsuit. L. deemed his wife's description accurate: "A very pretty, rosy complexion, jet black hair and a kind of cute, attractive face. She should lose some weight though." In person, he decided, she looked and sounded her age. It was the telephone, apparently, that took 10 years off her voice.

Ushered into a large kitchen at the rear of the house, he apologized for being late and, as they sat at the kitchen table, accepted the offer of a cup of tea. The kitchen and the adjoining family room were bright and well-scrubbed; an attractively furnished front living room had looked off limits to small children. Taped to the refrigerator door were a couple of drawings by a 4-year-old, and presently the artist himself appeared, trailed by a 3-year-old playmate and the artist's sister, less than a year and quite mobile on all fours. After introductions and treats, the boys went off to watch Sesame Street. The little girl played quietly in the kitchen.

While Mrs. D'Ark fixed the tea, L. talked with Marv, a sharp, practical fellow with middle-of-road politics. Responsible for his family and business, he was not in a position to join his wife's crusade, but he too apparently understood the situation in moral terms, supported her effort and seemed proud of her.

Mrs. D'Ark thought L. might be interested in seeing their wedding pictures and brought out a handsome album of large, full-color photos. A number, she said, included Rabbi Adler, and L. might even find, in some of the shots of different tables at the party, people who had been involved in the "squelching." She seemed to have a particular table in mind but finally decided the album didn't include a picture of it.

The wedding had been a large formal affair with hundreds in attendance at a downtown hotel. L. got a look at both sides of the family and noted several good shots of the rabbi. They seemed to capture what L. suspected was the man's dilemma on such occasions. Certainly, he had felt the moment's solemn importance. Mrs. D'Ark explained that she had postponed her marriage a full year, because Rabbi Adler, off on a sabbatical in Israel, was not available to perform the ceremony. She had to wait for his return. No one else could have married her. At the same time, the glittering social trappings, the small talk, the posing, the hours taken from study or writing or counseling may have caused a measure of frustration.

In the pictures Mrs. D'Ark seemed a calm and confident bride, and now in person her gaze was frank and steady. There was nothing unsure or tentative about her movements, L. thought, nothing shy or reticent or devious about her.

L. asked if the D'Arks had seen the new issue of Newsweek with its cover story on "The American Jew Today." Since they had not, he explained its premise: with new power, new pride and new problems, many Jews "feel they have entered a new phase in the perennial problem of coming to grips with their identity." It was a typical Newsweek concoction, he thought, seemingly comprehensive but remaining largely on the surface, touching most of the problems but neatly avoiding most of the real pain and confusion. Sure to flatter and reassure much of the American Jewish community, its most interesting note was sounded on a page devoted to the new self-regarding attitude of "The Jewish Establishment."

"Jews are justified in being nervous today," Norman Podhoretz, the editor of Commentary, was quoted as saying. "There has been a very definite increase in the visibility of American anti-Semitism." The implication was, as L. had been noticing for several months in Podhoretz's magazine, that American Jews today should be concerned first and foremost with their own interest. The page included a photo taken at a United Jewish Appeal fundraising dinner with Moshe Dyan at the podium surrounded by several Jewish celebrities L. recognized, including Henny Youngman, former Brandeis president Morris Abrams, and Detroit's most prominent Jew, Max Fisher, industrialist, philanthropist and civic leader.

Sitting in the kitchen sipping tea, JoAnn D'Ark felt it necessary once again to apologize for what her people had done to L. and his book. And once again L. said he could see no reason to feel that way.

"I can't understand how you can be so calm about all this," said Mrs. D'Ark. "I know how I would be if this had happened to me, and I'm amazed at how you don't seem to be bitter at all. Of course, I know that some people don't show their real feelings, and maybe that's what you're doing."

"No, I don't think that's what I'm doing," he said. "I really don't feel any bitterness. I mean I understand why this was done. I know these people aren't evil, that what they did was simply wrongheaded and mistaken and that it wasn't directed at me personally. I just happened to be the author of this book they were upset about. Really, I've been rather amused at my own reaction, which has been mostly a fascination with the idea that someone had the power to do this thing."

Later when the novelty had worn off, L. would occasionally find himself angered and bitter over aspects of the situation, but for the moment he felt relieved, even, as on the night he first heard the story from his wife, elated at the possibility that there might have been good reason beyond any failure of his own for the lack of response to his book.

Chapter 17

They talked around the D'Arks' kitchen table for more than two hours, and later in the week L. returned for another visit, this time bringing copies of reviews and letters. He wanted to outline for the D'Arks everything he knew about the fate of his book.

His first foreboding had come in the middle of last summer when Publisher's Weekly, a trade journal supported by the industry establishment, failed to list *Murder in the Synagogue* in its preview of books to watch for in the fall, a compilation based on publisher-supplied information. So these were the books seen by their own houses as having a chance to make it in some fashion in the coming season. Either there had been some mix-up or, contrary to what he'd been told, Prentice-Hall held low expectations for his book. Think positive, he advised himself.

Early in August, again in Publisher's Weekly, he found his first review. Books, he knew, were sent to the Weekly early, usually in galleys, in order to be reviewed soon enough to allow the use of quotes in launching promotion. Dealing with the entire swarm of new trade books, reviews in the Weekly were always brief and often kind. The notice on L.'s book read:

> On the morning of Lincoln's Birthday in 1966, a psychotic 23-year-old youth, Richard Wishnetsky, stood up and condemned the "phoniness and hypocrisy" of the congregation of one of Detroit's major synagogues. He then shot fatally one of the country's most prominent religious leaders, Rabbi Morris Adler, and while his parents in the congregation watched in horror, killed himself with the same gun. L. has earnestly interviewed virtually everyone who knew the ill-fated young man, commendably

trying to understand the forces that made him, in L.'s own view, a tragic figure symbolic of the alienation of much of modern youth. Unfortunately we are given a great amount of raw material for a portrait that never emerges clearly. L. seems to lack the storyteller's ear and dramatist's eye of a Mailer or a Capote.

The use of odious labels and catch phrases like "psychotic" and "...symbolic of the alienation of much of modern youth" and the comparison with Mailer and Capote, neither of whom had written a book much like his, were not surprising from an anonymous staff reviewer. The opinion that stung was that he had failed to present a vivid, intelligible portrait of Richard Wishnetsky.

L. knew the opinion held no genuine importance but could not erase the fear that it might help to set a pattern. The Weekly was one of three early-reviewing services—the others being the Kirkus Reviews and Library Journal—that influenced in varying degrees the sale of a book to libraries, its selection by book review editors, and its publisher's attitude. The 300 review copies Pat Neger had talked about were scheduled to go out in the last week in August. He would simply have to bide his time.

On August 17th he wrote to the Wishnetsky family to say that his book would be available to the public within the next few weeks. He had worked carefully to respect their privacy, he wrote, and initial response to the book from Mrs. Adler, Rabbi Groner, and others in the community had been highly favorable. He added:

"Naturally I hope that the book's publication will cause you as little discomfort as possible. I also hope that you might understand my feeling that the increasingly violent generational confrontation of the past four years has vindicated my original conception and intention in writing the book. If it helps even a few troubled young people and their anguished elders to see themselves, their world, and each other a bit more clearly, I'm sure we can all feel its purpose achieved."

Later he heard from two reliable sources, one of whom had spoken directly with the family, that the Wishnetskys had been surprised and upset by his letter. The book having taken so long to reach print, they had apparently decided that L. had been forced to abandon the project. Now suddenly the book was about to be published, and Mr. Wishnetsky was talking seriously about suing for an injunction to stop its appearance. One of L.'s informants, a man who had read the book, had argued against such action, telling the family they had nothing to fear in the book and that generally a new book was an object of attention for only six months or so, after which talk about it died away rapidly. A court suit could, in fact, intensify and prolong the public spotlight. The family, L. was told, took this advice to heart.

Also in August, L. exchanged letters with Tom Miller, Prentice-Hall's director of advertising. "Galleys have been sent," wrote Miller, "to Karl Menninger, Kenneth Keniston, Bruno Bettelheim, Leslie Siefer, Bernard Fiedler, Bernard Malamud, Sal [sic] Bellow, Philip Roth and Herbert Gold. As soon as we have some indication of their response we will write to the other individuals on the list that you sent us." The last four were novelists and had not been on L.'s list. Leslie Fiedler had apparently been split into Leslie Siefer and Bernard Fiedler.

As for the "launch campaign," Miller said he planned advertising in the New York Times, Hadassah Magazine, The National Jewish Monthly, and Judaica Book News, a catalogue produced by a New York wholesaler. He had also managed to secure an agreement with J. L. Hudson's, Detroit's largest department store chain, in which each would pay half the cost of an ad in the Detroit papers. L. told Miller he felt this approach did not touch some of the book's most obvious and potentially important market areas. In response Miller wrote:

> Please do not think that we only mean to sell this book to the Jewish community. The Times hits many more people than Jews, obviously. Your suggestions of Commentary, The New York Review Of Books and Psychology Today are periodicals which I would have suggested for a second time around too. Let's hope the book does as well as we think it will so that we can do some more advertising in that area.

Chapter 18

Early in September Tam Mossman sent L. a copy of a review in manuscript received at Prentice-Hall from Fredric Wertham. A psychiatrist regarded as one of the world's leading authorities on violence, Wertham had been on L.'s list of prestigious names; he had been sent a copy of the book and asked for a statement to be used in promotion. Wertham had responded with a full review soon to appear in the American Journal of Psychotherapy. L. had quoted Wertham in his epilogue, valued his opinion and quickly read through his review now, picking out his judgments:

"...stands out as a real achievement."

"...has the great distinction that it is the result of pain-staking investigation of the inner and outer circumstances of the case."

"...does not speculate and does not decide beforehand--as is so often the case--which data he will consider relevant."

"...very correctly realizes that this is not a complete explanation. He does not just add on the social dimension, but-presents it as part of the intrinsic picture."

"The data in this book have been collected with such meticulous care and are presented in such an undogmatic way that the book has enduring value. It is not enough to recommend this book; I should express the hope that it will be widely read, understood and heeded."

Beyond the strong approval from a widely recognized authority, the review included an accurate description of the book, implying the appeal and interest it might have in the intellectual and academic communities. Perhaps it would help Prentice-Hall to think more carefully about promoting the book in these areas. The review would appear in an important professional journal with a small but in-fluential audience, and its last paragraph would serve as an excellent quote in the company's advertising.

L. was still floating when the phone rang with a call from Rabbi

Groner at Shaarey Zedek to arrange the delivery of a copy of the book to the synagogue. After L. offered the news of the Wertham review, the rabbi rendered congratulations and asked about Prentice-Hall's promotion plans. With radio and TV, L. explained, he had more or less decided against making appearances. Frankly, he felt they wouldn't be needed in Detroit where interest in the story still ran high. With reviews and advertising in the local papers and perhaps a few notices in the national press, there should be enough word-of-mouth generated in the city. Besides the book just didn't seem to lend itself to radio and TV discussion.

"What I've really decided, " said L., rather taken with himself, "is to ask if a particular appearance might have some intellectual justification, and I doubt that an appearance on the Lou Gordon Show, for example, could have any." The rabbi said he agreed completely.

Lou Gordon, a tough-talking, muck-raking commentator and interviewer, had the most popular show on Detroit TV, 90 minutes on Saturday and Sunday evenings on a Kaiser network station. The Gordon show was considered one of the best book-selling programs in the country, and within a few months it would go national with syndication in the other Kaiser cities: Boston, Philadelphia, Cleveland, Los Angeles, and San Francisco.

Beyond the presumed local interest in *Murder*, the fact that Gordon and many in his audience were Jewish had made an invitation to appear seem likely. Then late in the summer, L. heard an amusing story that altered his expectations. At a dinner with relatives, his Aunt Nancy, a hostess at a west-side restaurant, said she had asked one of her regulars, the assistant producer of the Gordon show, if L. would be a guest on the show. No, said the young woman, since L. had said he would not appear on the show unless Lou promised to read the whole book beforehand. Of course Lou rarely had time to fully read any of the books whose authors he interviewed, so no, probably not.

L. was amazed. He had indeed said exactly that in joking with a few friends who were asking if he'd be going on with Gordon. And now his sarcasm had apparently somehow reached Gordon's staff. Basing program decisions on rumors was a strange way to run a show, he thought. But at least he knew that Gordon's staff was aware of the book.

A few days after L. received the Wertham review, a letter arrived from Prentice-Hall's subsidiary rights director, John Nelson. Replying to one of L.'s questions, Nelson wrote, "I think that it would be a mistake to bring an agent in at this point to handle any of the rights." L. had also asked Tam Mossman if it would be advantageous now to have an agent and had received the same answer.

L. knew the company would handle on its own any possible sale to a book club or a paperback house, but he did feel a bit vulnerable without someone in New York to give him the inside story and to watch out for his interests. If he wanted an agent to handle his future work, said Mossman, he should try a man named Julian Bach. But L. continued to feel so vague and uncertain about his future work that he put off contacting Bach or looking for another agent.

"We have submitted the book," wrote John Nelson, "to the first serial market without success. The book has gone to all the weekly supplements that we deal with, second serial market, book clubs, newspaper syndicates, all reprint houses and eight of our motion picture contacts."

L. thought the book's narrative was too long and complex to be serialized or excerpted. He was curious about the response of film people, but he was really only concerned about selling the book to a reprint house and perhaps to a book club.

About the latter Nelson's letter had good news: "We have just heard from the Commentary Book Club (Commentary Library) that they are interested in using the book. We are presently negotiating with them to see if we can come up with a mutually agreeable set of terms."

It had been a good week. First Wertham's review and now this. The Commentary Library was a relatively small book club, and the sale would probably not amount to many copies. But Commentary and its operations were owned by the American Jewish Committee, which was at the heart of the American Jewish establishment, and the club's selection of his book meant both prestige and publicity.

John Nelson also included information about the company's efforts to sell the book abroad and said they would "no doubt...result in the expression of interest by foreign publishers."

Chapter 19

L. brought copies of his book, each inscribed with a note of gratitude, to Rabbi Groner and Mrs. Adler and to the elderly attorney who had arranged his first interviews with them. The rabbi reiterated his high opinion of the book but said he had decided it would be appropriate for him to remain officially neutral on it, to make no public statement. With Goldie Adler he chatted warmly for two hours, after which the rabbi's widow filled a plastic bag with some of her freshly baked pastries for L.'s wife and son. The lawyer, an old colleague of L.'s father, had recently suffered a stroke that left him partially paralyzed, but he was as enthusiastic as ever about the book. He called L. a week later to ask that a copy be delivered to his old friend Philip Slomovitz, the editor of, the Jewish News, who wanted to review the book.

L. decided Pat Neger must have slipped up. Slomovitz should have received a request copy nearly a month ago. Joyce Carol Oates had probably also been neglected. In a letter on July 30th, L. had supplemented those two names he had previously given Miss Neger with the list she had asked for: a dozen people who might write or talk about the book. They had been mostly friends and contributors to the book toward whom L. felt some obligation, especially with the price at $9.95. Checking with some of these people near the end of September he found that none had received a book. Pat Neger was out when he called Prentice-Hall, but after a long wait while the answer to his question was checked, he was told that the author's request copies had definitely been mailed.

The first retail copies of *Murder in the Synagogue* had begun to trickle into some of the stores in Detroit, two books each at Doubleday's and B. Dalton's, a half dozen at the Northland J. L. Hudson's. One of the country's largest shopping centers, Northland served the heavily Jewish end of the metropolitan area, northwest Detroit and the northern suburbs. L., his wife, and friends watched most of the bookstores in this area and found that those few copies initially ordered disappeared within a week or two. Expecting something more, including, perhaps, prominent display, L. was surprised at the size of the first orders. And surprise would become dismay at the length of time the company would take to fill reorders.

By the end of September, with no word from Prentice-Hall, he had found the two remaining early reviews in the Library Journal and The Kirkus Service. Like the review in Publisher's Weekly they were necessarily brief, mentioned the thoroughness of his research, and surprised L. with their final judgment. The Journal reviewer (Henry M. Kapenstein, Free Library of Philadelphia) wrote: "L. has accepted and presented too many stereotypes as specific truths about Wishnetsky the Jew, a nervous bright-boy, an anxious, violent scholar, a naive know-it-all." The description was so blatantly false and unfair that the book must have touched some kind of problem in the man, thought L. Mr. Kapenstein suggested the book "For special-interest collectors only."

"Well, there's your first charge of anti-Semitism," said L.'s friend S., a Jew who had found the book "excellent" and "a very troubling experience." He added, "I hope you're not taking this kind of tripe seriously."

The unsigned Kirkus review was actually quite positive most of the way, with L. described as seeming "more psychologically aware of Richard's mood swing than the string of psychiatrists whom he saw..." A two-word parenthetical insertion in the final sentence, however, effectively undermined the impression: "L.'s recapitulation is to be read (by whom?) as a psycho-dramatic case history recorded in straight forward fashion without conjecture or censure — opportunities for both present themselves all along the way."

"We're certainly not going to sell many books to libraries," L. told his wife.

In the October 2nd issue of the Jewish News, Philip Slomovitz reviewed the book in a long, tortured piece that L. considered a confused but honest attempt to confront what had clearly been a painful experience.

> How does one review a book that deals with a murder in a synagogue, with the death of a prominent rabbi, with the mind of a lad who committed the crime and ended his own life;

with the sick boy's grandparents and parents who were so well known to the reviewer and the many characters in the book also known intimately to this writer?

Slomovitz described L. as a "good reporter" and much of the book's analysis seemed to win approval, but the man's overall attitude was reflected in two subsequent paragraphs:

> If it were fiction, if the characters had been distant, if all, not a few, of the people quoted and alluded to had been described as many are by L. as 'Psued.' — that the names used were pseudonyms — it would have been easier to accept this book. But the people are known, the tragedy is too near to us, that synagogue is where we worship--how can we accept it all with grace and say that the book is anything approaching pleasant reading?

> While Detroiters who were close to the scene of action and to the actors in this horrible drama will be saddened by what they read in L.'s account and some may be sorry it was written — there is inevitably great sympathy for the parents — there will be another sentiment: a regret that an evident danger in a declining mind was not checked in advance.

October 8th, the book's official publication date, passed quietly. By now L. was watching, with varying expectations, for reviews in Detroit's two dailies, the New York Times, and certain national magazines. Of course, even the seemingly comprehensive Times managed to review less than a tenth of the books it received, and the odds were considerably worse in other newspapers and journals. So one had to be realistic about the possibilities. Still, buoyed by Fredric Wertham's comments, he thought there was a chance of an occasional notice and was confident of a review in at least the local papers. By the middle of the month, however, there had been nothing in either the News or Free Press and no ad co-sponsored by J. L. Hudson's.

As for the New York Times ad promised by Prentice-Hall's Miller, L. found it not in the Sunday Book Review but in the middle of the book page for Monday, October 12. Four inches by two and a half, it carried the cover design, title, author, publisher and price and said:

> In 1966, Richard Wishnetsky used a sawed-off Colt .32 to assassinate Rabbi Morris Adler. Wishnetsky then shot himself. Why? The answers lie in this remarkable book--a double portrait of murder [*sic*] and victim.

Incredible, thought L. Wertham's statement had arrived a full month before the ad appeared, and they had not used it. He couldn't imagine how this ad would sell many books.

Chapter 20

Sensing a need for the personal touch, L.'s father brought a copy of the book to the Detroit News and sought out book editor William Silverman. Never seen nor heard of it, said Silverman six weeks after he should have received a review copy.

"What's new about it?" he asked unpleasantly.

L.'s father, somewhat taken aback, said, "Well, it's all new. It tells the whole story for the first time." Silverman agreed to take the copy and look it over.

The next day it was the Free Press, and this time an old friend, associate executive editor Frank Angelo, promised to see what he could do for the book. L. wondered if his father's approach might be less than helpful but wondered even more about Silverman's reaction at the News.

Near the end of October John Nelson finally wrote in answer to an inquiry from L.: "I am sorry to have to tell you that the Commentary Library has rejected *Murder in the Synagogue* for use in their book club." Since Nelson had originally said the club wanted the book, L. assumed the club had rejected not *Murder* but Prentice-Hall's terms for its sale. Knowing nothing about how such deals were negotiated, L. was nonetheless disappointed and sure the prestige and publicity value would have far outweighed any monetary disadvantage.

Also near the end of the month, L. finally got a phone call through to publicity woman Pat Neger. Two earlier calls and two letters had elicited nothing but silence. In one of the letters he had asked again about the author's request copies. "If these people aren't going to get books through you, then I really have to get copies to at least some of them in another fashion."

This he repeated now on the phone along with his concern about the scarcity of books in Detroit area stores and the failure to get review copies to the Detroit dailies and the Jewish News. Miss Neger apologized about the request copies and said they were only now going out. (They would finally be received well into November.) About the other matters she acted surprised and concerned, asking L. to list the area stores waiting for reorders and assuring him that she would check on the review copies for Detroit's papers, though she was certain they had been sent.

What about radio and TV? asked L. out of curiosity. Well, she had assigned the company's man-in-the-field, Bob Yoder, who worked out of Chicago, to visit the shows in Detroit, and in fact she would make a point of getting his report that very afternoon (a Friday). On Monday she would call L. back, she promised, and tell him just what Yoder had come up with. What about outside Detroit? Nothing much so far, though she recalled two or three expressions of interest; the CBC wanted to interview him as did a radio station in Philadelphia. L. was pleased about the CBC but would later learn that the offer had been the result of his mother sending a copy of the book to an old friend, who, it turned out, worked for the Canadian network in New York.

On Monday L. did not hear from Pat Neger about what she had learned of Bob Yoder's efforts in Detroit. In fact he would never again hear from Miss Neger on the subject.

A few days later, however, she did send along a review from the Lansing State Journal of October 10th. It seemed a bit strange that Lansing should have a review before the Detroit papers touched the book, but L. felt reassured that at least some review copies had gone out. The reviewer, someone named Christy Nichols, began by asking:

"Who doesn't remember the shock, on a February morning almost five years ago, of learning that a prominent Detroit rabbi had been shot during the Sabbath service in his synagogue...?"

She described the book as "a monumental task... carried...to satisfactory completion." And she ended with: "This book is important to Michiganders, to Jews, to Detroit's Jewish Community, to religious leaders, to psychiatrists and to all students of the alienated young. It is worth reading, too."

Chapter 21

To L.'s surprise, brief excerpts from 25 pages of the book's final section appeared in the November 1st issue of the magazine supplement of the Sunday Detroit Free Press. Clumsy editing had given no proper indication that material had been deleted and had produced inaccuracies. With a sentence or two missing, Rabbi Adler appeared not to have received a mortal wound. Still, L. felt there might yet be some hope for this book.

For a while he assumed that a company initiative had been responsible for the appearance of the excerpts. But months later the magazine's editor David Dolson would explain that L.'s book had come down with a note from Frank Angelo saying the author was the son of an old friend and asking if excerpts could be used. Normally, said Dolson, the paper's book review people watch for new books that the magazine might be able to use and send them on. But in this case he had not heard of L.'s book until the copy from Angelo had arrived.

After the treatment in the Free Press, a bit more talk began to filter back to L., often with remarks and questions like, "I haven't been able to find it anywhere," and "Does the library have it? I just can't afford ten dollars."

At the suggestion of its director, L. had donated a copy of the book to the community library in his thriving, heavily Jewish suburb - of Oak Park. A year and a half later there would still be a waiting list for the library's two copies. The director was a pleasant, helpful man whose wife, he explained, worked on the annual Jewish Book Fair at Detroit's Jewish Community Center. Would L. be interested in speaking at the book fair or perhaps to various groups in the community? The library occasionally got calls for information about speakers and would be happy to send people on to L., if he liked.

At the moment he was taking a wait-and-see attitude, said L., primarily because he had thought his book might spark some controversy in the community, and he didn't wish to appear in public in a way that might fan the flames in any direction. A better course, he thought, was a quiet one that no one could interpret as an effort to promote or exploit strong feelings in the community in order to sell his book.

The Jewish Book Fair, however, was an obvious place for the book, and Prentice-Hall's advertising guy Tom Miller promised to contact the organizers and make the book available. When the fair opened in November, however, *Murder in the Synagogue* was nowhere to be seen, and L. quickly chalked it up to another company mix-up.

Though it was only one full month past the publication date, there had already been too many mix-ups and failures to make him very confident about the support Prentice-Hall was giving his book. Recently his friend S. had asked, "Do you think maybe they got a phone call over there?" suggesting that the publisher might have been threatened with a suit by the Wishnetskys. L. had thought about the possibility but then dismissed it because: 1) he was sure the family had taken the sound advice given them to drop the idea of legal action; and 2) he felt the company's behavior could be more easily explained as a function of its judgment of the book's sales potential.

The same ad he had found in the Times had appeared in the October issues of the National Jewish Monthly and the Hadassah magazine. In the Judaica Book News the ad also contained a quote from the Kirkus review: "A psycho-dramatic case history recorded in a straight-forward fashion without conjecture or censure." The Sunday News and Free Press never carried the cooperative ad the company had supposedly arranged with J. L. Hudson's.

L. decided to call Tam Mossman in an effort to gauge Prentice-Hall's current attitude. Well, said Tam, as genial as ever, things had been a bit slow, but the company was not displeased. It would just take a little longer for the word to get out. No, the company planned no further advertising for the book before the first of the year. Early in the new year they would probably run a large ad for a number of their books including L.'s in the Sunday TIMES. But you never knew what advertising might do for a book. Frequently it did nothing. No, he thought it was too late for a review in the Times now. No, he didn't know about any other reviews or about the number of copies sold so far. He would ask his secretary to send that information along. No, he didn't know the size of the first printing. He would have to check on that himself.

L. would also ask about the size of the print run in the other departments he was dealing with at Prentice-Hall. No one had an answer.

Shortly L. received a note from Mossman's secretary saying that 2000 copies had been sold as of October 15th. This was for the most part a pre-publication figure, and though nominal, it was larger than L. had expected. As for reviews, there was only one new one, a long, highly positive assessment written by a man named Jack Riemer for the Here and Now Journal. Later he would learn that Riemer was a rabbi and a prominent reviewer of books of Jewish interest. In Reimer's review he found a line that would serve nicely as a quote in the ad he had decided to concoct for his own amusement: "a fascinating double-portrait of the Rabbi and his killer that holds the reader' spellbound from beginning to end."

First, he made a Xerox copy of the ad Prentice-Hall had run, snipped it in two, and pasted it up. Then he typed in the quote from Rabbi Riemer and another from Fredric Wertham. Four by four inches: not bad, he thought, certainly an improvement on what the company had used.

Chapter 22

For some time he had been thinking about going to New York and speaking directly with the people at Prentice Hall. Finally, he called Tom Miller in advertising and arranged for an afternoon meeting on the Tuesday before Thanksgiving. Helpfully, Miller said he would alert John Nelson in subsidiary rights and Frank Tooni in publicity.

On Monday, the day before his trip, he arrived home late in the afternoon to hear his wife announce, "S. called. He wants you to look at the TV guide for Wednesday morning at eight." L. did so and found himself listed for an appearance on the Morning Show, a locally produced 90 minutes of news and interviews.

Quickly he called WXYZ-TV in an effort to reach someone from the show, but the staff had already left for the day. He explained the situation to the station's receptionist, said he would be out of town tomorrow, and knew he would have to call back in the morning from New York.

Without thinking about it much, he knew that if the Morning Show was actually expecting him on Wednesday, he would choose to appear. That he would otherwise be leaving the show's producers in the lurch helped to ease his decision. But more important was the fact that few of his expectations had been met that fall in Detroit. Most people in the city had probably never heard of the book, and at the rate things were going, they never would. To clinch the argument he employed the inevitable rationalization of the writer: for at least this one time, it might be an interesting experience. He had seen the show only a couple of times, though it had vied successfully for years with such formidable competition as Today and Captain Kangaroo. Its host, a man named Bob Hynes, was probably the smoothest personality on Detroit TV.

If the show expected him, the company's man in the field, Bob Yoder, must have made the arrangements. And, if so, there had been another mix-up or failure. Having never received the call Pat Neger had promised, L. had assumed that she had nothing to report from Yoder. There was no way now that L. could sustain his first impression of Miss Neger as an efficient and reliable young woman.

On Tuesday morning at the airport, as they waited to board, L.'s father asked, "Is that the only coat you have to wear?" A large black car coat that somehow looked Russian to L., it had seen its best days when he was still a collegian. Yet he remained fond of its power to make a third generation Sicilian-American raised in Grosse Pointe feel like a character out of Dostoyevsky.

L. grinned at his father and said, "No, I have a couple of others, but I like this one. You know, Dad, I have to consider my image. Writers don't dress like you and me."

"Oh, I see," his father laughed.

The exchange was revealing. Not too many years back, words between them on the subject of L.'s somewhat seedy apparel would have been delivered with teeth slightly on edge. L. had grown up resenting the time his father had seemingly stolen from him to devote to the building of his large practice. When people had asked him as a child if he too were going to be a lawyer, he had always said, "No, I don't want to work that hard." And for a long time he had tried to repay his father with a lightly veiled scorn and aloofness, sure that his dreams of a life of art and intellect would never be understood by this practical-minded attorney.

His father had no doubt been hurt occasionally, but he continued to be patient and generous with his deliberately strange son, and L. had finally begun to understand this immigrant's son's devotion to his work as something more than a concern for material gain. The birth of L.'s son had brought them closer still, and the trend had continued after L. had started on the book, the first of his writing projects that had ever won his father's full understanding and approval. His father's contacts in the community and his financial aid — necessary though L.'s wife had continued to teach — had been indispensable in L.'s work on the book. He had dedicated the book to his father, who had quite naturally taken a special interest in its fate.

Now, though there was a large gap between them on many matters of culture and politics, they had learned to enjoy each other's company quite warmly by avoiding certain subjects and respecting limits on others. It was probably important to know, L. thought, that Richard Nixon, who personified for L. much of what was wrong with

America, could win the approval of a man as kind and intelligent as his father.

By 10 am, they had flown into La Guardia, rented a car, and driven into lower Manhattan where his father had a meeting to attend at the Amalgamated Clothing Workers Building on Union Square. In an office a few blocks way L. visited with a friend and made his call back to Detroit. Perry Krauss, WXYZ's young producer of the Morning Show, said L. had indeed been scheduled for tomorrow, but an hour ago, because of L.'s message about being out of town, they had cancelled him. L. explained that he planned to return home later in the day and would be willing to appear tomorrow morning if they still wanted him. Great, said Perry Krauss. Yes, he said, Bob Yoder had made the arrangements about three weeks ago. They had been expecting to hear from L. and were going to try to call him today when they got his message. No, a mix-up like this had never happened before with Yoder. He was a very reliable man.

After lunch L. and his father drove up to Englewood Cliffs. They were met by a secretary who ushered them downstairs to a large, low-ceilinged subterranean room honeycombed with a maze of carrels and small offices. Tom Miller was a tall, mild-mannered young man with a beard. L. guessed they were about the same age.

The three of them spoke together pleasantly for 90 minutes, during which Miller explained that his budgeted funds for the year had been spent, and no further ads could be authorized over the remaining six weeks. The company's plans for the new year were not yet set

He said the money budgeted for the cooperative ad with Hudson's was still available, promised to check with Hudson's about it, and agreed that if the store had reneged, L.'s father could pick up half of the tab so that the ad could be run in the News and Free Press for the holiday season.

When L. displayed his handiwork with the quotes from Rabbi Riemer and Dr. Wertham, Miller exclaimed, "I've never had an author make up his own ad before." He filed away a copy.

He admitted that galleys had not in fact gone to L.'s list of prestigious names, as previously reported. They had been sent only letters that described the book briefly and asked if they would care to see a copy and perhaps make a statement to be used in advertising.

There had been, said Miller, only one or two takers, though quite possibly Pat Neger had picked up the list later and sent out review copies.

Miller also promised to check on the lack of books in Detroit area stores — the three at Northland had been out of stock at one-point for seven weeks — and also in Ann Arbor, the setting for a good portion of the book, where it had not appeared at all.

At one point Miller asked John Nelson to come in with a report on subsidiary rights.

Well, unfortunately, said the smooth-talking Nelson, there wasn't much to report. None of the dozen paperback houses they had approached had shown any interest. And the same for the book clubs and the other outfits they had tried. He gave L. a work sheet to look over briefly.

L. asked: "What about the Commentary Library? Am I right in thinking that they did in fact want the book but couldn't meet your price?"

"Yeah, that's right," said Nelson. "They wanted to buy 2000 copies at a certain price, and we told them they would have to take 10,000. Otherwise we couldn't make what we had to on the deal. Of course, the real value would have been the prestige and publicity for the book..." Nelson's voice trailed off, perhaps as he remembered that this was L.'s point.

L. said he thought it unfair to view the book, as some seemed to, primarily as an entertainment. But Nelson interrupted to say, "Well, that's the way I see what I'm doing here. I'm selling entertainment. That's what I'm dealing in."

Nonetheless, said L., he hadn't written the book as an entertainment and felt it had a number of other qualities that could be effectively emphasized. He showed Nelson his ad and learned that the subsidiary rights director had not been aware of the Wertham review. With remarks like that, said Nelson, maybe he should submit the book to the Psychology Today Book Club and one or two of the social science clubs. Good idea, said L.

Both Nelson and Miller said according to what they had heard, the problem was that people had thought of the book as a piece of stale news, and they implied that this justified doing little or nothing for it. What it needed, said Miller, were some good reviews in the right places. Unfortunately, Pat Neger was not in today, and publicity director Frank Tooni was also out of the office showing Barry Goldwater, one of Prentice-Hall's other authors, around the New York media circuit. Miller said he would send a memo to Tooni asking him to check into the Morning Show mix-up in Detroit.

In the car on their way back to La Guardia, L. read through copies of four new reviews he had found in the publicity file. Two had been published in October in newspapers in Pomona, California and Fort Worth, Texas, and two in November in the Canadian Jewish News of Toronto and a reviewing service called Best Sellers. All of them were positive.

In Fort Worth the book was described as "significant on several levels" including "a look at Jewish life of remarkable scope and depth, of intimacy and charm." In Pomona the reviewer, a rabbi, concluded: "Though the book is high priced, it deserves to be read for its clear vision of the troubled times in which the Establishment and its young people seek to further the American dream." The reviewer in Best Sellers, a Ph.D., said more or less the same thing but with his own favorite jargon ("mentational styles," "idio-logic," etc.). According to the Canadian reviewer, the book was "bound to raise some probing questions about modern Jewish life."

Also in a day or two, Haskel Frankel's "Criminal Record" column in the Saturday Review would spend two inches on *Murder In The Synagogue* while treating seven other books: "...an admirable job of research...The result may strike the average reader as a bit overlong and over-detailed, but those with a psychological bent should find it fascinating."

On the plane back to Detroit L. told his father it was obvious that Prentice-Hall had given up on the book some time ago. Yet for a number of reasons, he felt better and was sure his trip had been worth the effort. At least he had personally told the heads of two departments what they should know about the book, and one way or another there would be a good ad in the Detroit papers before Christmas. There was a small batch of new reviews, and tomorrow morning he would talk about the book on Detroit television. Maybe all of this meant a new, more promising start.

Chapter 23

L.'s appearance on the Morning Show want well enough. His mother and his former kindergarten teacher both said so later, but then so did producer Perry Krauss, who asked him to stay around after his 20-minute interview, so they could have him on again in case another guest, the famed Dodge TV sheriff, failed to make it through the snow from his downtown hotel.

Perry Krauss had gone to school with Richard Wishnetsky and had known Rabbi Adler. He seemed genuinely interested in the book and asked L. to check with the company about the extra promotion copies the show should have received. Bob Yoder had been able to give them only one copy, which had gone to host Bob Hynes.

On camera, though he had not finished the book (having lost a day's reading with L.'s reported cancellation), Hynes had been sharp enough to avoid asking the simple question with the complex answer: "So why did Richard Wishnetsky kill Rabbi Adler?" Instead they talked about how L. had come to write the book, what the experience had involved, and why people might be interested in reading it. L. had felt relaxed in the way he had always felt for some reason in front of a classroom. He had remembered to wear a blue shirt instead of a white, he had not been forced to grope for a word, and he had not scratched himself in the wrong place. In all he thought he had given an accurate description of the book to people who might not otherwise know it existed. He had not spent much time on it and was not about to forge a new identity as a media star. He was not unhappy to see the sheriff arrive in time to make his appearance.

That afternoon he managed to reach both Frank Tooni and Bob Yoder by phone. Tooni had heard of the Morning Show mix-up but had not talked yet with Pat Neger. L. asked if other shows had been lined up; Tooni didn't know and gave L. Yoder's Chicago phone number. L. asked if publicity had sent review copies to the list of prominent names he had given to advertising. Tooni said how about if he sent L. a list of everyone to whom they had sent review copies? Fine, said L. Tooni obviously knew nothing about his department's effort for the book, but he seemed very friendly, especially when he learned they had been in Ann Arbor at about the same time.

Bob Yoder in Chicago explained that he had passed on all the details of the Morning Show arrangement to Pat Neger but didn't know what had happened after that. Had Yoder made any other arrangements? Yes, J. P. McCarthy's radio interview show wanted him, but later; they were filled up right now and would be back in touch. Yes, said Yoder, things were picking up now, and reorders were starting to come in.

Reorders had been coming in for months, thought L. They were only now being filled.

He had begun to send out copies of the book on his own to people whose work he admired or who seemed likely to find the book of interest, and in December he got his first two replies. From Bernard Rosenberg, on the editorial board of Dissent, author or editor of a number of books, and currently professor of sociology at the University of Chicago: "I read it in two long and bitter bouts, but with deep admiration throughout. From first to last you display a rare writer's gift for achieving empathy with people you did not previously know and for recreating a milieu many of whose elements must have been alien to your own experience."

And from Edwin Shneidman, professor of medical psychology at UCLA and one of the country's leading experts on suicide: "It is clearly one of the most thorough 'Psychological Autopsies' that now exists. It is by every measure and from every point of view a terribly sad story and you have handled it well and in a most sensitive manner."

L. put copies of the two letters in the mail to Prentice-Hall, then wrote to Shneidman asking if he would permit his remarks to be quoted in advertising. The professor promptly agreed. Rosenberg, who said he was planning to visit Detroit (his hometown), L. would ask in person.

Three weeks passed without word from Tooni about those who had received review copies or from Miller on the fate of the Hudson coop ad. After two more unreturned calls, L. finally reached Pat Neger and told her of Tooni's promise to supply a comprehensive list of review copy recipients. Oh, that would be a lot of trouble, said

Miss Neger, since such a list would have to be typed up from a collection of individual slips. Why didn't L. give her the names he was wondering about, and she would check on them? L. did so and finally learned that none of these people had been sent the book. Miss Nager said she would mail him ten copies from their stock in the office to reimburse him for those he had been sending at his own expense.

As for the Hudson ad, when L.'s father finally spoke with the head of the store's book department, he was told that it had been put off until at least after the first of the year. L. tried unsuccessfully to reach Miller, then arranged to place his ad on the book pages of the Sunday News and Free Press for December 20th. Ten days later he sent copies of the ads to Miller with a letter saying:

> It seemed to us plainly advantageous to advertise this book before Hanukkah and Christmas, so we went ahead even though I couldn't reach you. I wasn't pleased with the typography in either ad, but they may have had some effect: I know of two stores who sold about a dozen books during the following week. You'll recall we talked about your doing a coop with us if Hudson's backed out. Can you still do that? The ads totaled something under $400.

L.'s father felt they had a legally binding verbal agreement. But in a letter that passed L.'s in the mail, Miller explained that Hudson's had "simply cancelled" the coop ad and that the publisher would be "unable to participate in any more advertising on the book," including the coop ad. Miller's letter was in effect Prentice-Hall's post-mortum on the book:

> I'm sorry to have to write you on such an unpleasant note. I hope you understand that we thought the book had strong potential — otherwise we would not have published it. But even though the book seems to be selling fairly well, it does not seem to have found a significant enough market in the most obvious marketing area for me to justify any more house advertising on it. This is simply an economic

decision and no reflection on your book, of
course.

Chapter 24

Of course, thought L., it's just that Prentice-Hall has this strange way of treating a "strong potential" book in its "most obvious marketing area" — not bothering to send out request copies or to check on the lone coop ad scheduled until it was too late, failing to tell the author of the only media appearance arranged, and taking months to fill book store orders.

After he had twice complained, through the latter part of November and all of December, the book seemed to move into and out of several stores in the area at a good pace. After the holiday rush, however, it began to disappear from the shelves as demand dwindled apparently and reorders stopped going out. A month or so into the new year the book was difficult to find, though a few copies would linger in the city for several months. According to a number of bookstore clerks, the price had been a major problem.

In December an acquaintance sent L. a clipping of a highly favorable review — "A searching and exhaustive study...illumined with penetrating psychological insights" — published in the Minneapolis Tribune complete with a blotchy picture of the author and written by an old friend and colleague of Rabbi Adler. And in January he learned of a notice in the Windsor (Ontario) Star, published across the Detroit River but not sold on the American side, and another in the Boston Globe.

The Canadian reviewer called the book "remarkable" and wrote: "He deals with the Jewish faith and Jewish environment with great understanding and sympathy and with such knowledge as to make it difficult to believe he was not reared in that faith." In Boston the reviewer, though writing with a generally positive tone, claimed that L. seemed "to blame the bankruptcy of our society as the major factor in Richard's decision to carry out this dramatic assassination-suicide." It was the same kind of misreading that L. had found on the book jacket.

A few months later he would learn of three more reviews that had praised the book in December and January: in the Allentown (Pa.) Labor Herald ("brilliant"), the Kansas City Jewish Chronical ("well worth reading"), and the Dallas Times Herald ("surprising, sobering and frightening"). In all, with help from Prentice-Hall's clipping service, he would find more than fifteen highly favorable reviews and only three with a tone suggesting, the reader should save his time and money — the three brief preview reviews in Publisher's Weekly, Library Journal, and The Kirkus Service.

But L. was puzzled most by the odd distribution of notices across the country, in places like Pomona, Allentown, and Kansas City. Frequently the "provinces" took their cue on books to treat from the early reviews and the Eastern press, but in this case the early reviews had been less than favorable, and in New York with its Jewish population larger than Israel's, there had been no mention at all. As for Detroit, he had decided well before his January visit to Rabbi Kapustin and the Hillel center that someone of influence had suggested to the News and Free Press that it would be best for everyone involved if the book was not given attention. In any case, with two reviews in the Dallas-Fort Worth area, he often told friends, "Yes, but I'm a hot topic in Texas."

Early in January the letter from Robert Coles arrived in which the widely respected psychiatrist and soon-to-be Pulitzer Prize winner explained that he had been "absolutely enthralled" by the book. Again L. wrote back for permission to quote from the letter, which Coles quickly granted. By now, some four months after its appearance, most of L.'s fears and doubts about the book's value had abated, and he realized that his embarrassing need for positive feedback and reassurance had been largely a result of his inexperience. In writing the book he had been forced to explore a wide variety of material with as much fresh intelligence as possible — certainly a valuable experience but, even in retrospect, at times unnerving. Helpfully, the response he was aware of in the Jewish community, though not the extended discussion he had hoped for, had been almost uniformly positive.

It was not difficult now for him to believe that he had written a good book, even one that had surpassed his hopes in significant data and readability. And in the months ahead he would receive more letters from people whose opinions were important to him. The famed psychiatrist Karl Menninger called it a "beautiful book" and suggested it might "help people realize how complicated crime is." One of L.'s former professors said he thought it "might well become a classic in personality psychology case study." And a Canadian sociologist called it a "first rate contribution to studies of socio-pathology."

What L. could not believe was that his effort had been genuinely tested in the intellectual marketplace.

He had begun the book for a number of reasons. One had been his sense that many young people were falling prey to the notion that social and historical forces were producing an unprecedented assault on individual identity in post-war American society. The temptation was strong, he thought, to rationalize away the need for personal responsibility and individual struggle and to see oneself as a victim of large societal forces, driven to aberrant and anti-social behavior, which in itself would serve as evidence of the culpability of society.

As much as anything else, the Vietnam war and his feeling in 1966 that it was rapidly fostering a climate of alienation and rage among the young had impelled him to tell this story. And as the appalling violence and the generational confrontation of the last years of the '60s unfolded, he thought the book's purpose had become only more relevant.

But when publication finally came, in the first year of the new decade, he felt the national mood had shifted. The public had become surfeited with media accounts of violence, with books and articles on mass murders, assassinations, riots, and atrocities, and with studies purporting to give historical, sociological, psychiatric, or biological perspectives on all of it. Americans had turned away to their new obsessive contraries: the romance of Erich Segal and the anti-romance of women's liberation; the irrationality of the occult and the scientific study of ecology.

Yet despite such a climate and the odds against any new book by an unknown author, L. finally felt his book could have found a market if the publisher had made a reasonable effort to support it. Why Prentice-Hall had not made such an effort—considering the amount money and time it had invested in the book—he could only explain by turning to the popular notion of bureaucratic incompetence in the publishing business. Despite all his efforts to educate the company about the book, his words had apparently never impressed those few at the top who made decisions. And once a book had been written off up there, one could not expect the underlings to pay it much concern. Unfortunately, this was a view that meshed only too well with L.'s skeptical and ironic turn of mind.

With a sour smile he recalled the whimsical note he had jotted to himself and chuckled over during the preceding summer: "I fear I'm going to come charging out of obscurity only to go racing off into oblivion."

Chapter 25

On the newsstand in February he found in the new *Writer's Yearbook* a piece called "Does Advertising and Promotion Sell Books?" by Sol Stein. Three points caught his eye:

1) "That is why some publishers work so actively to get each of their titles considered and hopefully chosen by one of the 100 or more book clubs in the United States. It is not just for the immediate profit of a book club sale, but for the effect the book club distribution will have on word-of-mouth."

2) "It is very important that [the author] plan for the program, with the help of the publisher's promotion director, carefully and at length...TV and radio interviews [are] the most important and effective forms of book promotion today..."

3) "A comparatively small number of reviewers—actually fewer than a dozen—influence most book buyers and so a publisher must devote a great deal of his promotional effort in fighting for each one of the titles he publishes with each of the reviewers who count—persuading, cajoling, and finally, if he gets a good review, merchandising it, by reproducing hundreds or thousands of copies of the good review and sending it out to bookstores and elsewhere so that people in all areas will know what is happening in one area."

Right, mused L., who had been thinking about using comments from Drs. Wertham, Shneidman and Coles and two of the rabbis in an ad of his own in the New York Review Of Books and Commentary. He learned that a good-sized ad in each would cost less than those he and his father had placed in the News and Free Press. And he was still thinking about it when his wife came home that February night with the improbable news of her chat with JoAnn D'Ark.

PART III

Chapter 26

L., who often moved only after considerable self-prodding, watched with admiration as Mrs. D'Ark bustled into action. The day after their first meeting she drove to the Wayne State campus at the center of the city to speak with Rabbi Kapustin. She had been terribly upset about what had been done to this book, she told the rabbi, because of how the action reflected on the Jewish community, contravening, as it did, basic Jewish values she had cherished since childhood. And since her information had come directly from the man responsible, she felt duty-bound to act in some way to help reverse the injustice.

Well, he had no such first-hand information, said the rabbi, but if she did, her desire to act on it was laudable. Mrs. D'Ark told her story in detail but maintained the agreed upon fiction that she had not yet approached L. She explained that though she felt she should first contact the author, she feared his reaction to the news. That was no problem, the rabbi assured her; he had talked at length with the author and was certain the reaction would be calm and reasonable. He urged Mrs. D'Ark to get in touch with L. asap.

Would the rabbi agree to vouch for her character if she used him as a reference in some of the approaches she was planning to make? Of course, said Rabbi Kapustin.

The next day she called the Harry Golden at his home in North Carolina. Golden, the old journalist who had been a favorite of Mrs. D'Ark's, seemed interested in the story she told him and asked for a copy of the book. A day later L. mailed him one along with Mrs. D'Ark's short follow-up letter which included Rabbi Kapustin's name and address.

Over the weekend she kept busy, calling relatives in different parts of the country to ask if they had seen or heard of the book, and reaching the wealthy and influential old family friend in New York who could get L. on the Cavett show. The old man had failing eyesight and would need the book read to him, but he would be back in touch shortly. Two weeks later he would agree with Mrs. D'Ark on the book's merits; though it was too "intellectual" to have mass appeal, he thought, he would do what he could for it if Mrs. D'Ark succeeded in getting the pressure removed from the publisher.

Also during the weekend she confronted her father with the news that she had gone to the author with her information. She had not divulged the name of the man responsible, she explained, nor had she involved anyone besides herself, but she was bound and determined to set matters right by going to "Uncle So-and-so" and doing whatever else was necessary.

"Well, there was this explosion," she told L. later. "But I was expecting it, so I just braced myself. I knew that he knows me well enough to understand that when I say I'm going to do something like this, I mean it. So I just let him fume and yell at me for a while, and then I said I was hoping that he would help me. And after a while he said, 'All right, so what do you want me to do?' And I said, 'How about getting him on the Lou Gordon Show?' And he said, 'Okay, you want him on the Lou Gordon Show, I'll get him on the Lou Gordon Show.'"

On Friday, she explained, he was planning to see a friend and business associate who, as one of Gordon's closest friends, would smooth the way. In the meantime he had asked her to hold off going to "Uncle So-and-so" until he had thought a bit about the best way of handling that end of it.

Though even now L. was not pleased with the prospect of appearing on the Gordon show and would have preferred the quickest possible confrontation with the man responsible, he felt that things had to be done Mrs. D'Ark's way, and now, it appeared, at least for a while, her father's way. He was happy to gain another ally but a bit confused about the father's role in all of this. Originally Mrs. D'Ark had voiced suspicions that her father had been involved in the effort against the book, yet she was hoping to secure his aid. He had advised her to come to L. before going further, yet now he appeared to be shocked that she had told L. what she knew. Only later would it occur to L. that JoAnn D'Ark had quietly hoped to prove her father's moral integrity and that he in turn must have thought his daughter's plan was simply to help the book by getting it some attention, certainly not to drop her explosive information into the author's lap.

Chapter 27

The new week saw Mrs. D'Ark still moving quickly in her effort to find allies among those who had been a part of the High Holiday gathering, as well as among rabbis and others in the community who might be in a position to help in some fashion. She was not successful.

People at the gathering either denied having heard anything or made it clear they had no intention of doing anything about what they had heard. Others who had not been at the gathering said they knew nothing of the matter and could see no way to help. One rabbi, the leader of a small, ultra-liberal suburban congregation, said he could certainly ask L. to come and speak as part of their lecture program, though at the moment they were booked up for several months.

JoAnn D'Ark told L. she was upset and disillusioned, because others apparently did not feel the urgency of the situation as she did. L. tried to put himself in the place of those she was approaching and wondered how he would react.

Impatient, they decided the story should be told to someone who already thought highly of the book. Mrs. D'Ark wanted to reach other Jewish writers, and L. suggested Bernard Rosenberg. He explained who Rosenberg was and gave her a couple of the man's recent articles to read. Fine, said Mrs. D'Ark, and with what L. thought was remarkable chutzpah called Rosenberg at home in Chicago. She explained who she was, told him her story, referred to his writing, and said she had not yet approached the author with her information. Though L. had quickly come to feel this deception served little purpose, he had decided that, since she would use Rabbi Kapustin as a reference again, they should remain consistent. On the phone Rosenberg, like Rabbi Kapustin, urged her to go to L. with her story and opined that L. could be trusted to react reasonably. Afterward L. thought this reassurance had probably been helpful:

JoAnn D'Ark had, after all, made no solid commitment as yet and was probably happy to get another independent assessment of L.'s character.

But as Rosenberg told L. later, he had not known quite what to do with this woman with the little-girl voice and the bizarre story who had seemingly called him out of the blue. ("You mean you've read the book? Oh, I don't believe it! What a coincidence!") And he had suggested that they all get together for a chat when he visited Detroit in a couple of weeks.

L. also thought about a call or a letter to Norman Podhoretz at Commentary. After all, Podhoretz, a man of considerable influence, had started everything by publishing L.' s original piece on the shooting at Shaarey Zedek and later, when L. had written to him for advice during the editorial battle with Prentice-Hall, had called L. long-distance at his own expense. The call had been delayed and had come after the matter had been settled, but it had been nonetheless appreciated.

Yet L. decided against an approach to Podhoretz now, because a recent exchange of letters with the editor indicated that, though the Commentary Library had wanted the book, Podhoretz's own response to it had not been positive. A few weeks back L. had written to ask Podhoretz's opinion of Julian Bach, the agent Tam Mossman had recommended. Actually L. had spent most of the letter talking about how the book, though praised by certain prominent people, had been generally ignored. He was, of course, fishing for some indication of Podhoretz's attitude, but in a quick little return note he got it only indirectly. Bach was probably as good as anyone for L., said Podhoretz without mentioning the book at all.

L. had finally sent a letter, a copy of the book, and some reviews to Bach in New York, and now a few weeks later he received a note from the agent saying, "You did a superior job in and with *Murder.* Do call me at your convenience." On the phone L. said nothing about Mrs. D'Ark's story, and Bach explained that what had happened to the book was unfortunate but not uncommon. With one or two reviews in the right places, it might have done very well. Yes, he was interested in selling the book's subsidiary rights as well as seeing L.'s short fiction. He was going off on vacation for three weeks, but he would look for some of L.'s short stories on his return, and they would talk again later.

A few days into March, L. received his first royalty statement from Prentice-Hall, for the period ending December 31, 1970. The statement indicated a regular bookstore sale of 1402 copies. The other categories were listed only with dollar amounts, but apparently about 80 copies had gone to foreign and mail order sale and perhaps something under 1000 had been discounted at 50% or more. The total came to not much more than the figure he had been previously given (2000 copies as of October 15). Total earnings for the author, most of it at 10%, came to $1941. With his advance deducted along with company typing and duplicating expenses of $241, L. was still $6800 in the hole.

At least it's not a debt, thought L., and he wondered what kind of a loss the company had taken. Months later with enough information to make an educated guess, he would come up with a figure that was close to the amount of his advance. A substantial sum but nothing to get too excited about for a company that grossed $128 million in 1970.

Chapter 28

It was the middle of a Wednesday evening two weeks after JoAnn D'Ark had first acted on her conscience. L.'s wife, having put their 7-year-old son to bed, walked into their living room to find her husband sprawled on the couch, his feet planted on the coffee table, talking on the phone with Mrs. D'Ark. Glancing up at his wife, L. pushed the button of his ballpoint and wrote something on the top margin of the New York Times Magazine cover featuring a painting of psychoanalyst Alfred Adler. Then he held up the magazine with a smile, and his wife read his large graceless scrawl: "It's Max Fisher."

Opening her well-shaped mouth and raising her neatly plucked eyebrows, L.'s wife sank into the nearest wing chair where she sat for the next half-hour listening to L.'s side of the conversation. Afterward he told her he thought Mrs. D'Ark had finally decided to give him the name primarily because she had been reassured about L.'s possible reaction and was disappointed that apparently little had been accomplished after two weeks. She had wanted to prove her continuing concern, a desire strengthened each time an awkward reference to "the man you heard" or "this man" was necessary in their conversation.

Mrs. D'Ark had begun with a note she had sounded before—her feeling that at least a few of those he had interviewed must have known about what was going to be done to the book and her disgust that L. had not at least been given a friendly warning. L. couldn't think of anyone he would put in such a category. The effort against the book had been initiated well after he had finished interviewing people. Still, Mrs. D'Ark had wanted to explore this possibility. She would give him a list of names and wanted him to say if he had interviewed any of them. These were people, she emphasized, who might have been involved: she had no evidence. She gave. L. seven or eight names which he jotted quickly across Alfred Adler's broad forehead. A few he recognized, but he had interviewed none of them.

Well, having gone this far, said JoAnn D'Ark, she might as well tell him the name of the man responsible. L. had probably guessed anyway, and there was little point in going on the way they had. When she announced the name, he felt like a puzzled schoolboy who had rejected the correct answer for what he had thought were good reasons. "Really?" he asked.

"Sure. You mean you didn't guess? Who else could it be?"

"Well, I don't know. Of course, his was the first name I thought of, but I figured he was too big. I mean I didn't think he would have any interest in something like this. No matter what was in the book, it wouldn't hurt him, so why get involved? When I think of Fisher, I think of some jet-set entrepreneur; I don't even associate him that closely with the Jewish community. And I didn't know he had any connection with Congregation Shaarey Zedek. Is he a member?"

"Oh, sure. He's a member of other congregations too, but he belongs to Shaarey Zedek."

And so began L.'s education on the subject of Max Martin Fisher, a process that would cover several months, though for a long time L. would remain only casually interested, not bothering with more than the occasional newspaper story about the man. L. had always made a point of being bored by tales of big money and the men who spent their lives involved with it, and he wasn't about to change now that one of these men had apparently touched his own life. Only much later, when L. would finally decide to write about his experience, would he make an effort to search out information on Fisher.

And only then would he begin to understand just how feasible the deed had been. For a long time he had wondered what kind of pressure or leverage Fisher might have used on a company like Prentice-Hall. But upon learning in some detail of the extent and influence of the man's holdings and connections, he would rule out anything as crude or explicit as the direct application of pressure or the use of a threat. The squelching could simply have been asked for and received as a favor from one businessman to another. It was enough that Fisher and some of his closest personal friends controlled some of the largest corporations in America and that if even one of these outfits decided next year to switch to another house for their business and technical texts, newsletters, and bulletins, Prentice-Hall's profits might suffer a crimp. It was not good business to make a man like Max Fisher unhappy.

Chapter 29

The Royalty of America hold their fiefs and titles
in corporate tables of organization. Their coat of
arms is the product logo; the banners of their
troops the colorful packaging containers. To be a
King Arthur is to head a company listed on the
Big Board; Sir Lancelot, American-style, is an
assistant to the President and a Dukedom is held
by a vice-president with substantial stock holdings.

But if their opinions hold sway in the affairs of
men beyond corporate boundaries, they are at a
rare strata indeed. They have become Princes of
the Realm, men who are their own personal base
of power.

Detroit's Prince of the Realm is Max M. Fisher.

If this noble and beneficent image of the titans of American
business seemed absurdly over the top, L. had to remind himself that
it had been intended quite seriously by those who had authorized it,
those wealthy conservative Republicans who owned and operated
the Detroit News. Over the past several years the publishers of the
News had done their best to keep their good friend Max Fisher, the
country's leading individual contributor to the Republican Party, in
the limelight properly accorded royalty.

The description of Max as Prince had opened their most ambitious
effort, a long, glowing profile replete with full-color photos that had
appeared two years back (February 23, 1969) in the News' Sunday
magazine. More recently the paper had done a major spread on what
it called "the Ten Biggest Wheels" in Detroit, the city's ten most
powerful men as chosen by a panel of prominent citizens. The 63-

year-old Fisher had been photographed on the phone in his office, his feet propped on his desk in the foreground, a hole in a sole, in a pose reminiscent of that famous shot of Adlai Stevenson. A panelist had been quoted: "He is not content simply to provide money for charity. He must involve his being; he must lead. He is supremely energetic and diplomatic. He's brilliant and deeply spiritual."

A few years back Max Fisher's business credentials had listed him as a major stockholder sitting on the board and on the finance committee of Marathon Oil; a board member of the Michigan Consolidated Gas Company and Michigan Bell Telephone; a director of the Safran Printing Company, the Fruehauf Corporation and Allen Industries; an investor in various Broadway productions and in theaters in both Detroit and New York; an investor in various foreign ventures including oil; and chairman of the Fisher-New Center Company whose real estate holdings included the landmark Detroit office building named after another (unrelated) Fisher and the giant $150 million Somerset Park apartment complex in the northern suburb of Troy. L. was sure the list would be considerably extended today. His friend S., a businessman in the city, said Fisher's reputed personal worth was pushing $100 million.

But it had been in his role as civic leader that Fisher had become Detroit's most prominent Jew. In 1968 he had raised $910 million for New Detroit, Inc., .a blue ribbon committee of business and community leaders formed after the 1967 riot in Detroit "to provide a positive thrust for the regeneration of our community and a 'piece of the action' for Black America." He had become New Detroit's second chairman and had announced that his goal was revolution, within the system, needless-to-say.

A year later he had left New Detroit to help form and serve as chairman for a similar organization called Detroit Renaissance, which was now concentrating on promoting development of the city's riverfront and was spending heavily on numerous radio and TV commercials intended to encourage Detroiters to think their city was "getting better all the time." For both organizations he was described as "a working, active chairman, not a name-lender." Department store heir Joseph Hudson had recently been quoted as saying: "Not many people get away with saying 'No' to Fisher, and he has a vision of what needs to be done."

And then there was Max Fisher, the international philanthropist.

The News profile described him as a "chairman, president, a director or vice president of 14 different organizations devoted to charity, hospitals, education, trade and professional interests." Some of these included the United Foundation, Detroit's Sinai Hospital with its new $1,000,000 Max Fisher Wing, the Council of Jewish Federations and Welfare Funds, and the Reconstituted Jewish Agency. He had helped to raise tens of millions for the State of Israel and other Jewish causes.

One example of his fund-raising L. found in Booton Herdon's book *Ford*. Herdon described Fisher as "a man of perception" and quoted him frequently on the subject of his close personal friend, Henry Ford II. At one point he mentioned a cruise that Max, Henry, and food magnet Nathan Cummings had taken with their wives on the Aegean at the time of the Six Day War:

> Fisher, who has been an adviser to the Israeli government since the state was born, was naturally deeply concerned. As a former president for several terms of the national United Jewish Appeal, he is familiar with fund-raising and helped organize the Israeli Emergency Fund. Naturally, as he was emotionally involved, he discussed the situation with his friends, but he deliberately refrained from taking advantage of his friendship with Ford to ask for a donation.

Herdon wrote that Fisher had shown him a short note he had later received from Ford "handwritten on his personal stationery":

> Dear Max:
>
> Enclosed is a donation to your cause. I had meant to do this much earlier, but I feel that, with the continuing problems we discussed the other evening at your house, you will continue to need substantial funds....
>
> All the best,
>
> Henry

Ford had enclosed a check for $100,000.

Next to Israel, Fisher's favorite charity was the Republican Party. A long time personal friend of George Romney, he had been the chief fund-raiser for Romney's gubernatorial campaigns in Michigan and for his abortive try for the presidency in 1968. Then after Romney had given up the effort in New Hampshire, Fisher had turned his allegiance to Nixon and had contributed a total of $105,500 to the cause, channeled through 37 separate state and national fund-raising committees. It was the largest sum received by the Party from an individual contributor.

There had been much talk lately of how big money men in America were buying political power. But a recent Free Press article had quoted Fisher as saying: "Every citizen, to the extent of his means, has the responsibility to do his best as a citizen. A person who gives 50 cents, if that's what he can afford, is just as important as someone who gives $100,000." Of course, when America's sweetheart couple, John and Martha Mitchell, had visited Detroit recently for a political stage show, they had stayed the night not with the man who had given 50 cents but with the Fisher family in their suburban Franklin home.

"It is no secret in Washington," the Free Press story had said, "that Fisher's words on Mideast policy carry weight with the Nixon administration.

"He was asked if large political contributions are important to obtain that kind of entree to power to talk about arms for Israel or the oil depletion allowance.

"Fisher said: 'I can express myself whether I give a dollar or $100,000.'"

But when Richard Nixon had looked for someone to serve as a special adviser to the president on urban and community affairs, he had tapped Max, not a one-dollar contributor.

The published information L. would finally assemble on Max Fisher would contain few personal details, and all of them would come from that deeply reverent profile in the News:

> He comes in a big size. You can look at him and see a Buckeye varsity center in that large, husky frame. When he talks, you feel the power of the man in the steady voice of command pitched so low that you must sit forward in your chair and listen carefully.

His dark, brooding eyes will capture you, as will the mobile face with its large, worn, sorrowful expression. There is a patriarchal quality about his face in repose that reflects a huge capacity for understanding.

When the pace of business quickens, you can catch the reflection of acquisitive ambition and sense the driving energy that has brought him from a small town boy out of Salem, Ohio, to the counsel of presidents and Heads of State.

So that was where it had all started, in a small town in Ohio. But what in his childhood or upbringing might account for the man's enormous drive for status and the exercise of power? There were no indications given.

In 1930 he had graduated from Ohio State, where he had played some football apparently, with a degree in business administration. It had then taken him 27 years—as "a pioneer in the history of oil in Michigan," working first in waste oil, then founding and developing the mid-west's largest independent producer of petroleum products, Aurora Gasoline, buying out a large distribution chain called Speedway 79, and finally in 1957 selling the whole thing to Marathon—to make his first million.

The News piece described him as a man of "intense dedication," "tremendous self-discipline," and "complete honesty" who "works and plans 10, 20 and even more years ahead" and "has the ability to use power well." It spoke of his "extreme shyness; his innate sense of dignity that extends beyond himself to others; his ability to scan-read, digest and retain volumes of data." And it said that "a rare period of depression...is almost always due to a feeling of frustration when he knows the solution to a problem and must wait for others to reach the same conclusion."

Somewhere back in the murky days before the first million, there had been a marriage that had turned sour, divorce and remarriage to a divorcee. Frequent world travelers, Fisher and his wife lived with their two teenage daughters in their home near the lovely rolling fairways of the exclusive Jewish country club, Franklin Hills. There were three older children from the other unions, including pretty Mary in her early twenties, a favorite of the society columnists.

According to the News, Max Fisher's day started at 6:30 each morning, and by the time he reached the office he had already dispatched a pile of business on the car phone. "What comes home after the business day is pretty near dead sometimes," his wife was quoted as saying. There had once been a yacht to relax on, but according to his wife he was too busy with community service now to bother with recreation. He frequently, however, indulged a passion for cowboy movies in his private mini-theater at home.

Only once would L. find a hint in the NEWS profile of something else behind the image of benevolent shyness, dignity, and restraint in this man who had spent 27 years mounting his first million and had then used the next 14 to do it again perhaps 100 times over. "When taking issue on a point, he stands tall before you, arching back on his heels, his right hand flicking out, jabbing home each point with his forefinger. His voice alters then, and you don't have to lean forward to hear him."

Even so, L. would decide there was no point in trying to reconcile published reports with a remark he had heard recently from a friend whose husband was a young millionaire businessman in Detroit: "From what I hear, Max is known around the locker room at Franklin Hills as the biggest son of a bitch in the city."

Chapter 30

On the phone to Grosse Pointe L. told his parents the news, and though they didn't know Fisher personally, they sounded sad and disappointed, almost as if they had been betrayed by an old friend. The advice from his father remained more or less the same:

"Go along with this woman and see what happens. Let her take the lead and do what she wants to do, but see if you can get something in writing from her." It was doubtful, he said, that much could be done legally even with a signed statement from her, but without it there was no hope at all.

On Thursday night at the community college, L.'s wife asked JoAnn D'Ark how Max Fisher could have been careless enough to talk in public about what he had done to the book.

He hadn't really been careless, said Mrs. D'Ark, because he hadn't really been in public. You had to understand, she explained, that there were really two Max Fishers. There was the public Max Fisher, the carefully modulated civic leader who knew about manners and good taste. But there remained also the Max Fisher of the early days, before he had become a public figure, the hard-driving businessman who liked to let his hair down with a gathering of old friends and talk the gossip of profit and loss in the old rough and ready way.

After dinner at a gathering like this, she continued, the women always went off in one room and talked about what women talk about, and the men always went into another, smoked cigars, and talked business. She had always followed the men, said Mrs. D'Ark, because she had always found their conversation more interesting. Sitting there in a corner, she generally just listened and took it all in. So on this particular evening Fisher knew very well that he was speaking only with long-time friends and old business cronies. And, of course, he had known JoAnn D'Ark since she was a little girl. There had been no conceivable way his remarks could be transmitted to the wrong people — until some months later when Mrs. D'Ark's conscience had prompted the inconceivable.

As L. understood the matter now, having talked at length with JoAnn D'Ark, the idea had probably originated not with Max Fisher but with that small handful of wealthy members at Congregation Shaarey Zedek for whom it was enough that the book would air again the charges of materialism and hypocrisy and would spotlight the pain and embarrassment caused by the shooting. Perhaps they had sat around with Max and had wondered aloud about what to do. Perhaps they had gone to him directly as the man with the most power in his pocket.

Mrs. D'Ark felt their motivation had also involved a fear that the book might contribute to a rise in anti-Semitism, and later she would suggest that concern for the Wishnetskys might have been a further consideration. L. would continue to see both factors as secondary, perhaps little more than rationalizations. The Wishnetskys' reportedly strong reaction to his letter announcing the book's appearance (coming several months after the approach to Prentice-Hall would already have been made) convinced him that the family had played no role at all.

About this time L. received in the mail a brochure from Arthur J. Goldberg inviting him to become a member of the American Jewish Committee, sponsors of Commentary and probably the country's most prestigious organization of its kind. Perhaps someone from the Committee had seen the book and assumed he was Jewish, thought L., as he read through the impressive list of prominent members. Near the top of the Committee's hierarchy, in fact just below the name of its current president, the Board Chairman of the National Executive Council was listed as Max M. Fisher.

Chapter 31

Though L. had vowed to maintain a skeptical attitude toward Mrs. D'Ark and her story, he had been unable to find a solid reason to doubt either her integrity or her tale. He had established with certainty that she was the person she had said she was and that she had accurately described her connections with family, friends and Congregation Shaarey Zedek. He had spoken with her almost daily for nearly three week now, had seen her interact with her husband and her children, had talked alone with her husband about her, and had badgered his imagination to come up with an alternative to the inescapable impression that she was a sane and dependable woman who was telling him the truth.

The imaginable alternatives — that she was attempting to deceive him for some vindictive or insane reason or was honestly deluded herself — seemed absurd, for in either case she had already placed her family, including her father, in line for considerable unpleasantness if L. decided to act in some fashion that would make the story public.

From talking with Marv D'Ark L. knew the husband was well aware of this possibility and concerned about it. But, though Marv said he was worried about JoAnn's health — recent tests had indicated that she might be suffering again from the illness that had nearly taken her life as a teenager — and concerned about the pressure she was under, he continued to support her effort. Given the positions of both the husband and the father, their obvious fears and allegiances, both personal and social, L. was certain that if either man had harbored the slightest doubt about the full truth of Mrs. D'Ark's story, either or both would have quickly called L. to say so.

As for JoAnn D'Ark herself, L. had come to see her as a woman with a fierce, uncompromising sense of justice and a strong need to speak her true feelings. She had a good, droll sense of humor and an instinctive shrewdness about the motives of people. But there was also a provincial ignorance of some of those outside that small, well-insulated group she had grown up in, a failing that she was quick to admit and scold herself about. Used to the cosmopolitan Jews who had been among his closest friends since his university days, L. was surprised by the prejudice she would occasionally describe in herself. "I really used to think," she had said at one point, "that most Gentile husbands beat their wives."

She was devoted to her children and her husband, but they were not her only interest in life: she was not sitting around her suburban ranch with time on idle hands. Besides caring for the children, cooking, washing and cleaning house, she was fund-raising for her son's Montessori nursery school, taking college courses at night, lecturing at Weight Watchers, and, with her father's "head for business," nearly as much involved with her husband's firm as he was, frequently serving as both secretary and consultant. And more than once when L. had called her too early in the morning, she had explained, her voice still heavy with sleep, that she had been up half the night with a good book.

A letter from Harry Golden arrived at the D'Ark home stating politely that Mrs. D'Ark's story could not be true. No group of Jews would ever do such a thing, he reasoned, because if the plot were ever to become known, the sales of the book would increase a thousand-fold. JoAnn D'Ark felt Golden was telling her: "I have no interest in getting involved, but if you want to help the book and think you have the facts, make them public."

L. had not yet heard from Rabbi Kapustin and finally decided it was time to call the Hillel director. It was a bit of a touchy situation, he thought, since there might be certain powerful members of Congregation Shaarey Zedek who could, if they wished, put the rabbi's job in jeopardy. Nonetheless, he had not finished explaining that he was calling about a woman he had met recently with information about his book, when the rabbi interrupted to say yes, he had spoken with the woman and had advised her to get in touch with L. He had wanted to call about it himself but had unfortunately misplaced L.'s phone number.

L. asked what the rabbi could tell him about JoAnn D'Ark.

Well, said the rabbi, she had been a student of his about ten years ago, and he knew her to be a very forthright person. "You see," he said with his slight German accent, "I had suspected for quite some time that all was not right with your book. And you may recall that back in January when we talked here, I said something to that effect."

"Yes, I recall."

"Well, I have no knowledge of what was done or by whom, but I did feel there was something wrong. Normally, with a book like this one, I would get an advance word on it in maybe six or seven places; publishers send me notices on their new books; other groups and organizations send me information on these things. But with this book I never heard a word. I heard nothing about it at all until a friend of mine in the Religious Affairs Office here showed me his copy."

"So in other words, Rabbi, you would advise me to listen carefully to this woman?"

"Listen carefully, and step carefully," said Rabbi Kapustin.

"And it would be your opinion then, having known her for several years, that Mrs. D'Ark is not the kind of person who would make up a story like this, that she's a woman of integrity and responsibility?"

"Integrity and responsibility, yes. Of course, as I told you, I have no knowledge myself of what was done, but let me put it this way: I am morally certain that what she says is true."

Chapter 32

Other than his parents L. told no one but a couple of friends about the tale he had heard from JoAnn D'Ark. His friend S., a brilliant, emotional man, offered his outrage along with a steady stream of advice and moral support, all of which L. greatly appreciated.

"I'll tell you what you should do," said S. "You hire yourself the meanest, toughest son-of-a-bitch lawyer you can find, and you have him go to Max Fisher and tell him a few things. Not your father because your father's probably too nice a man, and he's too emotionally involved. But somebody who knows how to deal with Fisher and his people and isn't afraid to get tough with them."

"But I wouldn't know what to ask for from Fisher. He doesn't have anything I want."

"What about bread?"

"But how much would be appropriate? Anyway, I don't want any of Fisher's money. And what I want even less is all the hassle and unpleasantness, all the rotten publicity and ugly feelings that a court suit would mean. Besides, my father says a suit for deprivation of rightful income, or whatever it would be, is the worst kind of case to prove. All I really have on Fisher is Mrs. D'Ark's word and no way of getting anything else. And all I've got on Prentice-Hall is a lot of circumstantial evidence which the company could easily pass off as the kind of mix-up and miscalculation that's very common in the publishing business."

L. knew that his father had been deeply upset by what had happened to the book and would like nothing better than to use his profession to win some kind of redress. But with the insertion of Fisher's name in the story, his father had seemed increasingly pessimistic. Beyond the difficulty of gathering any further solid evidence, he said, JoAnn D'Ark herself could be placed under such intense pressure that it would not be safe to rely on her as a legal witness.

R., another friend who had thought highly of the book and a

woman who occasionally wrote for some of the country's leading intellectual journals, argued that it was naive to think that a man like Max Fisher could be made to undo what he had done through a moral exhortation or the threat of exposure from someone like Mrs. D'Ark. The man would consider himself just too big to be concerned about such things.

No, the only thing to do with a situation like this was to expose it as quickly and as effectively as possible. L. should have JoAnn D'Ark write out her story in full and then supply the rest of the details himself. R. would then write a cover letter and perhaps offer to review the book and send it all off to Robert Silvers, the editor she knew at the New York Review Of Books. She wasn't sure what Silvers could or would do with it, but she thought he'd be interested. And if he did publish something on it, the Review would be the best possible place for an expose.

The idea had considerable appeal for L., but he still wanted to try settling the matter quietly first. Fisher held a lot of power, but he also seemed a man much concerned with image, particularly his own. And if he thought it in jeopardy, he might respond.

And do what? R. wanted to know.

Well, at least he might lift his pressure from Prentice-Hall, said L., so the company could do something intelligent to promote the book and at least get it into paperback. Besides, I would prefer not to see this story break over the Jewish community with all the misunderstanding and ill-feeling that would be generated.

There wouldn't have to be a lot of misunderstanding if it were done right, said R., a very knowledgeable member of the Jewish community, if the blame were laid properly at Max Fisher's feet, and it was made very clear that most of the Jewish community had known nothing about the action and would no doubt denounce it.

L. filed these ideas away for future reference, but for the moment Mrs. D'Ark was running the show, or rather her father was. The latest word was that he had seen and spoken with his friend who was close to Lou Gordon but had not had a chance to ask about getting L. on the show. Then a few days later JoAnn D'Ark called with the news that her father had come up with a new plan. Why not go to Gordon directly, he had suggested, and give him the whole story? Gordon had no use for these people and didn't care whose toes he stepped on, and he would love a story like this.

If Gordon got involved, then JoAnn could give him all her information, and Lou, as he often did, could keep his source confidential. That way she could step out from under all the pressure and could avoid the trauma of a showdown with "Uncle Max." Gordon, with all the facilities at his command, would be in a better position to use some real muscle.

JoAnn D'Ark was clearly pleased with her father's plan, and, though L. had both questions and misgivings, there seemed nothing for him to say except, "Well, let's see what happens."

Chapter 33

L.'s Jewish friends were making discrete inquiries, and it would soon become clear that the salient elements of Mrs. D'Ark's story were not common knowledge in the community, and that even within the congregation they had probably been voiced to very few. But then, thought L., even if someone had heard the talk, unless they, like JoAnn D'Ark, had heard it directly from the man responsible, their information was little more than gossip, hearsay or rumor, and as such, nothing they could properly act on.

Rabbi Kapustin, for example, might have been in this position, and if so, his words to L. on the phone had certainly been as far as he could or should have gone. In fact, thought L., considering the rabbi's position, he had acted with courage in urging Mrs. D'Ark to inform L. and in serving as a character reference for her. As for those few who had shared in Mrs. D'Ark's experience of hearing the word from Max Fisher himself, L. wondered without resolve what he would do if an old friend had made a similar statement in his presence. Friendship and group loyalty were naturally potent considerations.

In the meantime, at L.'s suggestion, JoAnn D'Ark had been writing out her story in a letter to be sent to Fredric Wertham and Robert Coles. L. had sent off his own letters to the two psychiatrists, telling them about Mrs. D'Ark, explaining the publishing details, and asking for advice. Mrs. D'Ark wanted both L. and his wife to appraise and criticize her writing, which they did, but the letter remained in all essentials her construction and accurately reflected her personality. As it was sent to Wertham it read:

> Because I know you have read *Murder in the Synagogue*...I would like to tell you a story that has been of deep concern to me for some time now.

First of all, let me briefly describe myself. I am a housewife and a mother of two pre-school children. My father is a prominent member of Detroit's business community, and I was brought up in the late Rabbi Morris Adler's Congregation Shaarey Zedek. Frankly, I must tell you that I am a totally unassimilated Jew in both thought and action. But something has happened here in Detroit that involves Mr. L., and I feel I must try to reverse an injustice done to this man and his book.

The knowledge that Mr. L., a gentile, and therefore an "interloper," was writing the troubling story of Rabbi Adler's murder had upset many people because they felt it might have a detrimental effect on the Congregation and the community. I had heard the talk, but it wasn't until the High Holidays, when I sat in on a conversation, that I began to think seriously about the subject. The essence of what I heard was that one of the men, particularly wealthy and powerful, had used his influence with Prentice-Hall to see that this book would be "squelched." He went on to say that he had been assured by the publisher that every means they had would be utilized to accomplish this. Someone asked how, and he said, "By not advertising the book, setting the price too high, etc." I thought that not selling the paperback rights would be another effective way to kill a book. It was also mentioned that the important New York reviewers would not deal with this book.

My first reaction beyond being fascinated at the power of some people was indifference. But the conversation kept returning to my thoughts and I couldn't reconcile my first reaction with my belief in Judaism and the thought of Jews doing something like this. I hoped the book would be a horrible disaster, written by an incompetent hack, so I wouldn't have to worry about the problem anymore. But after I read the book, I knew my knowledge of the situation would not leave me alone until I had done something.

I began to seek out any information I could find concerning the book to see just how, and if indeed, this book had been effectively suppressed. I talked to several Rabbis (one of whom independently confirmed my knowledge of the situation), and some prominent Jewish authors. At first, I didn't want to contact Mr. L. because I did not know him, and I feared what might happen if he capitalized on my knowledge. However, Rabbi Kapustin of the Hillel Foundation at Wayne State University and Professor Bernard Rosenberg of the University of Chicago had personal knowledge of the author, and they both assured me he would not do anything rash with my information. I have since spoken to him, and he gave me the un-happy details of what has happened to the book.

There are two reasons why I feel the injustice committed against this book and its author must be reversed. Both reasons are important enough to me to do anything I can to accomplish this reversal.

When I was a teenager I became seriously ill. Although many people tried to help, it was Rabbi Adler who gave me the strength, in fact, the very will to keep on living. I don't think two people can go through an experience such as this without feeling some kind of bond, and in the subsequent years I saw the many facets of Rabbi Adler's personality, both good and bad. With the perception and insights of a great writer, and the accuracy and objectivity I feel only a non-Jew could have given this subject, Mr. L. has written a truthful portrait, and in doing so, a great tribute to Morris Adler.

The second reason is because I love the Jewish religion and the Jewish people. The basic tenets of our religion are based on dealing with others in a just and truthful manner. Since these are the values that make my life worthwhile, I feel that my knowledge leaves me no alternative but to defend these values. The suppression of this book was accomplished by a few Jews who felt they were doing the right thing. I know they are not bad people, but I also know what they have done is wrong.

I have not mentioned the name of the man most responsible because I don't wish to expose what he has done, at least until my father and I have talked to him and given him the chance to re-verse his actions. I hope that when he realizes how deeply committed I am--if I am forced to, I will tell the whole story to the author, including names--he will at least release the publisher from his pressure.

In the meantime, I would be very grateful for whatever help and advice you could offer.

Mrs. D'Ark closed with this: "Finally, if you would like some confirmation of who I am and what I am doing, please contact..." Below she had listed Rabbi Kapustin and his address and phone number at Wayne State.

Chapter 34

At mid-morning on Thursday, March 11, JoAnn D'Ark called L. to say that her father had telephoned minutes earlier with the news that he had just spoken to Lou Gordon. He had supplied her with a phone number and said Gordon was waiting for her call. "Well, I'll tell him anything he wants to know," reiterated Mrs. D'Ark, "except the names of the other people at that gathering."

A few minutes later, she was on L.'s line again, this time sounding puzzled. "He didn't give me a chance to tell him anything," she said.

Gordon had been abrupt on the phone, she explained, had offered her little chance to supply more than a few details of her story. "He said, 'Before I can do anything, I'll have to have a copy of this book,' and he wanted to know if I could get him one. I said I was sure I could, and he said, 'Why haven't I heard about this book? Why didn't my staff receive a copy?' He seemed real annoyed about that, and I said, 'Well, that's an interesting question. That's just the kind of thing I'm talking about.'"

"But didn't he ask any questions?"

"Well, he asked about my motivation. He said, 'What's your interest in all of this?' And after I told him, he said, 'But what about the First Amendment? What about the right to free speech and the freedom to publish?' And I said I hadn't thought very much about that, which is true, I haven't."

"Did he seem to know the facts of the story already?" asked L. "I mean maybe your father filled him in before you called."

"I couldn't tell, but I don't think so. He didn't seem to know much about it."

"Did you tell him it was Fisher?"

"He didn't give me a chance. When I tried to give him information, he just stopped me and said, 'You want me to try to do something about this, don't you?' And when I said yes, he said, 'Then get me a copy of the book. I can't do anything at all until I read the book.'"

"All right, so we'll get him a copy of the book."

Mrs. D'Ark said she wanted to deliver it personally to Gordon's office at a time when she would have a chance to give him more details. She called her father who told her that early the following afternoon was probably her best bet, because he had been told that Gordon was always in the office at that time on Fridays. L. offered to drive her to Gordon's downtown headquarters and arranged to pick her up shortly after noon the next day.

In the meantime L. typed out a two page, single-spaced letter to include with the book going to Gordon. In it he described his healthy advance, the problems and delays with Prentice-Hall's editors and lawyers, the raise in price, the company's failure to promote the book despite excellent comments from important sources, the absence of reviews in Detroit and other logical places, the company's refusal to sell the book to the Commentary Library, its delays and failures in filling bookstore orders, sending request copies, and informing him of radio and TV arrangements.

For all of these dismal details, he explained, he had blamed the "stupidity and incompetence" of his publisher—until he had met up with JoAnn D'Ark. He recounted Rabbi Kapustin's recent comments on Mrs. D'Ark's credibility and added:

"Actually I don't know what could be done for the book at this rather late date, but I'm primarily concerned with two things right now: one, that this unpleasant story should not break over the Jewish community here unless it becomes absolutely necessary; and two, that the book be given at least a chance to reach a softcover edition where it would be available at a reasonable price. I do fear that if pressure has been applied effectively, the sale of subsidiary rights is unlikely."

With the letter he included copies of the ad he had placed in the News and Free Press and of another that had just appeared in the Jewish News. The latter, with brief quotes from Robert Coles, Edwin Shneidman, and Rabbi Mandel of Pomona, he had placed so that Mrs. D'Ark could use the quotes in talking about the book without having to reveal that she had spoken to the author. At least that ruse is over, L. sighed, though one small element of deception remained: he still wasn't supposed to know the name of the man responsible.

On Friday L. picked up Mrs. D'Ark, drove her downtown,

dropped her in front of the David Stott Building (Gordon's office was near the top) and picked her up again at the front entrance shortly thereafter. She had only been able to drop off the book and the letter, she said, and had been told that while Gordon was usually in at this time, today was an exception.

On the freeway back to the suburbs JoAnn D'Ark said, "You know, in all the talking we've done in the past few weeks, I've told you a lot about me. But I hardly know anything about you."

"What would you like to know? Ask anything at all."

"Well, the other day you said something that really shocked me. You were talking about how you had transferred to U. of M. after you had been at Notre Dame, and you said that after you'd been at U. of M. for a while you had fallen in love with a Jewish girl. And I just had the funniest feeling. I mean I assume if you were in love with her that she was in love with you, and that really shocked me. Not because it was you, of course, but that this Jewish girl had gotten that involved with a gentile. I mean I know it happens, but feeling the way I do, I guess I can't understand how it could. I don't think I've ever known anyone who's done it."

L. replied that many of his Jewish friends had married non-Jews and mused again over the remarkable fact that this woman had reached out of her world to help him.

Chapter 35

The following morning, Saturday, L. received a phone call from Lou Gordon. For the first three or four minutes he wasn't certain he was really talking to the city's biggest TV hotshot. The voice seemed too smoothly modulated. On camera Gordon was often raucous, his voice rasping and whining as he played his self-appointed role as defender of the little man against the wiles of big business, monopolizing utilities, and corrupt politicians. L.'s friends called Gordon a vulgarian, and L. agreed. But his feelings about the man were more complicated than that.

He recalled times on the show when Gordon's voice had responded to certain respected guests with an affectation of culture, and it was this note he was getting now on the phone.

After a few minutes the voice relaxed and became unmistakable.

Gordon explained that he had been very impressed with the honesty and sincerity of L.'s letter and wanted to go over some of the details. They worked through the letter quickly with Gordon reading over certain passages and L. briefly elaborating.

Said Gordon: "When you say here, 'Frankly, until very recently I thought of these dismal facts as probably standard authorial complaints and chalked them up to the stupidity and incompetence of my publisher--of which I'd been given ample evidence during my unpleasant battles with their editorial and legal departments.' I'm wondering if maybe all these things you talk about, all these terrible mix-ups and problems, could have resulted just from the publisher doing a poor job on the book. I've had my experiences with publishers too, and I know how bad they can be sometimes."

Said L.: "Well, that's what I had decided, more or less, until Mrs. D'Ark came along. And ever since, I've tried very hard to find some reason to doubt what she told me, but I just haven't been able to. I've investigated this woman and her background very thoroughly, and I'm convinced she's telling me the truth. And as I said in the letter, a man like Rabbi Kapustin has told me she's a trustworthy and responsible person and that he is 'morally certain that what she says is true.'"

L. asked about Gordon's familiarity with the book, and Gordon maintained that he had never heard of it until Mrs. D'Ark's phone call, and to his knowledge no one on his staff had been aware of it either. L. wondered if Gordon had been given any details by Mrs. D'Ark's father. Gordon said he had never spoken with Mrs. D'Ark's father.

"Oh, I thought you had. He told her he had just finished talking to you before calling to tell her to call you."

"No, I've never spoken to him," said Gordon casually enough that L. believed him. "And this woman called when I happened to be very busy and couldn't give her much time."

"Yes, she mentioned that. She said you were rather short with her and wouldn't give her a chance to tell her full story."

"Well, that's probably true. I guess I was short with her. But she caught me right in the middle of something, and I just didn't have time to give her."

"Of course, the important thing about her story," said L., "is that it's not a matter of rumor or hearsay. She says she got her information directly from the man responsible. And she quotes him directly telling this gathering at the High Holidays back in October that he had squelched this book—that was the word he used, *squelched*—and saying that the publisher had promised to do whatever was necessary to limit the sale and public discussion of the book. Things like raising the price, dropping advertising plans, and making sure that the important reviewers didn't deal with the book."

Did L. know the name of this man? Gordon asked. And L. lied, explaining why that information hadn't been passed on yet. Gordon wondered aloud if it could be So-and-so and named another wealthy member of Congregation Shaarey Zedek, a business associate of Max Fisher and a man L. had interviewed. "I've had some business dealings with him," said Gordon confidentially, "and I think he's a pretty shady character."

"Well, I don't know," said L. "But Mrs. D'Ark says she's willing to tell you the whole story including the man's name. And if I were you—if I may make a suggestion—I think the most effective route would be to call her up and get together perhaps, and just find out what she knows."

Gordon wanted to assure L. that he was definitely going to follow up on this matter and had in fact a great interest in it, not only because of the possible violation of the first amendment but for personal reasons as well. Please don't repeat this, he told L., even to Mrs. D'Ark, but he had never had much use for these people at Congregation Shaarey Zedek. He had been raised in the congregation and had known Rabbi Adler ever since the rabbi had come to Detroit. He had never thought that highly of Adler, always preferring what he felt was the more authentic style of Adler's predecessor, old Rabbi Hershman. But matters had really come to a head when Gordon's father had died, and after the funeral some of the leaders of the congregation had approached him about becoming a member. They would give him a special deal, they had said, and he would only have to pay the minimum required for the privilege of membership. He had been shocked, said Gordon, that anyone would have to pay to join a synagogue, and instead had offered to donate more money than the leaders had asked for to a fund that could be used for people who might want to join but didn't have enough money.

"Well, they passed on that idea, and so I passed on them," said Gordon. And he recalled having some understanding of Rabbi Adler's young assassin in his indictment of the congregation as a collection of hypocrites and materialists.

Gordon said he was anxious to read L.'s book but unfortunately would not be able to get to it immediately: there were three other books he had to read in the next week or so—Bill Moyers was coming in next weekend along with a couple of other authors. In the meantime, however, he would do some checking around ("I'll give Bill Silverman at the News a call.") and would get back in touch in the near future.

L. hung up surprised and even pleased with the call. Generally Gordon had sounded honest and interested, offering confidential information and expressing a personal, deep-running concern. Certainly this was Gordon's kind of story, he thought, the kind of sensational expose he appeared always on the prowl for. In fact, if aired, it would be the biggest splash he had made in years.

In L.'s view, Gordon's popularity and success had stemmed basically from the man's keen instinct for his audience. Some years back Gordon, an ex-insurance salesman, news reporter and clothing wholesaler (he was still in the clothing business) had apparently sensed in many a gathering distrust of authority, a deepening suspicion of presidents, mayors, policemen, professionals, experts, and leaders of all types, along with growing feelings of impotence and frustration. It was a commonplace observation of the American mood, but Gordon had cashed in on it, his popularity reaching new marks with the widespread disillusionment of the late '60s.

His favorite targets were organizations and groups he could indict collectively with a cavalier sweep of the hand: the current administration, the legal and medical professions, and the utilities. He inveighed often against the corrupt power of big business but was usually careful about going after individuals or companies. His muck-raking had never had much demonstrable effect, and his one claim to national fame had involved something else: it had been on Gordon's show that George Romney had committed political suicide by announcing that his brain had been washed on Vietnam.

Still, there were many who waited faithfully each week for Lou with his heady egotistical air to pin the rap on their gouging doctors and lawyers, lying politicians, and the greedy Michigan Bell. Of course Gordon dealt in vulgarity, taking a popularly prudish position on what he called "dirty books" but invariably presenting their authors to his audience, frequently offering catch-phrase answers to the most complicated problems in the style of a wiseacre kid of sixteen. The man's passion for controversy and his blunt-minded positions on complex issues such as crime versus law and order seemed more often to inflame feelings than to shed light.

And yet a compassionate and humane note ran through much of Gordon's commentary, and in recent years he had learned the helpful, trick of laughing at himself occasionally. To his lasting credit he had spoken early and with a continuing rough eloquence against the U.S. role in Vietnam.

The question now, however, was just how close Lou Gordon was to Max Fisher. L. could recall clearly only one instance in the past few years in which Lou had mentioned Fisher, and on that occasion his strongly critical remarks on the way New Detroit, Inc. (of which Fisher was then chairman) was allocating its funds had been prefaced with the line: "Now Max Fisher is a good friend of mine, and I think he's a well-intentioned man, but..."

There were other questions too. For example, was it possible that

117

Gordon's staff had kept their boss ignorant of a book likely to be of interest to him? Improbable, thought L., and he recalled again the strange story of how Gordon's assistant producer had said that the show would not approach L. apparently because of a flimsy rumor that L. would not appear on the program unless Lou read the whole book.

And why had Mrs. D'Ark's father sent her to Gordon with her information, if, as L. assumed, the man wished to keep the matter as quiet as possible? The idea had been that Gordon would work behind the scenes, but this seemed unlikely to L. It just wasn't Gordon's style. It was also supposed to protect Mrs. D'Ark from a confrontation with "Uncle Max," but that didn't seem a very good bet either. And what did Mrs. D'Ark's father know about the quality of friendship between Max and Lou? And why did Mrs. D'Ark's father tell her he had spoken with Gordon when Gordon denied it?

L. wanted to discuss all this with Mrs. D'Ark, but it was Saturday, and the family would not be answering the phone. Still, in case of an "emergency" on the Sabbath, he had been instructed to call, let the phone ring twice, then hang up and call again. This worked, but after reporting his chat with Gordon to JoAnn D'Ark, he continued to have no answers. There would be little time to ponder his questions, however. New developments were already brewing.

Chapter 36

On Monday morning JoAnn D'Ark called L. to say that her phone had been ringing since early Sunday evening: Fisher or people representing Fisher wanted to make a deal.

Mrs. D'Ark was calm but obviously pleased as she related the details. She couldn't say who had made the approach or had acted as intermediary, but L. strongly suspected it had been her father. The deal was that if Mrs. D'Ark would promise not to reveal Fisher's name to L. or anyone else, then the pressure on Prentice-Hall would be lifted and reviews would appear in certain places. What about carrying on with the kind of thing she had been doing? Could she continue to send out the kind of letters she had written to Wertham and Coles?

Yes, there was no problem with that as long as she didn't include Fisher's name. "Well, that sounds pretty good," said L. brightly. "I mean we're not really giving up anything if you can still go on spreading the word, and, of course, since I already know it's Fisher. I suppose they want some time to get the reviews arranged. Did they say where these reviews were going to appear?"

"No, but I told them that you didn't care too much about the newspapers and popular magazines and were more interested in seeing the book reviewed in some of the smaller intellectual journals. They said to give them two months, and then if we didn't see a real change, I would be free to tell you who it was, and we could do whatever we wanted."

L. said two months sounded reasonable but reminded Mrs. D'Ark that while he had thought the reviews most important to him would probably have come in the smaller journals, he had also speculated that reviews important to the book's sale might have appeared in certain major city newspapers and national magazines if all things had been equal. Also he thought there were certain assurances they should get from these people before they agreed to anything.

For one thing, he thought it would be fair to ask for a letter from Prentice-Hall that would give some indication that these people had in fact gotten back to the publisher. Not, of course, anything stating this explicitly, but simply a note saying the company had some new plans for the book and were going to run an ad, for example, in the New York Review Of Books or Commentary. Also there was Mrs. D'Ark's credibility to think about. If she was going to continue sending out letters telling her story, she would have to be vouched for. And it seemed unfair to make Rabbi Kapustin carry the load alone. Perhaps she should try to get assurances that one or two other prominent people acquainted with her would attest to her integrity, people who could not be pressured into sabotaging her efforts.

Mrs. D'Ark said she would get on the phone to these people, but she doubted they would be very forthcoming, especially about this latter request. In the meantime, said L., he would get in touch with his father, talk things over, and then get back to Mrs. D'Ark with his decision on the deal.

L. was still cautiously optimistic in describing the situation to his father, who agreed that the offer sounded all right as long as L. could get the assurances he wanted. "Let's see what they say and think about it some more," he said.

But as L. continued to think about this so-called "deal," the more he felt there was something repugnant and false about the whole business and something that angered him.

He found distasteful the idea that the same people who had seen to it that reviews did not appear, would now, with a similar use of power, see to it that they did. This was not what he wanted for his book, and it occurred to him again that no matter what happened from here on, there was no way he would ever know how his book would have done on its own under normal circumstances.

He was angered by what he felt had been Fisher's sheer effrontery, the sense this man must have had that he somehow had the right to meddle in other people's lives, to manipulate the outcome of their work for his own ends. But it was the ends themselves, as L. saw them, vain, wrong-headed, and foolish, that raised L.'s ire to the use of expletives. Max Fisher, he was sure, had delivered many a speech on the purity of the profit motive, and in praise of the free enterprise system. But, of course, Fisher, like many other American Merchant Princes, didn't really believe in the unfettered opportunity for any product to reach its market in fair competition.

Perhaps that was to be expected. But there had supposedly been some real concern for the good of the community as a whole and not just for the image of the congregation. Yet now it seemed Fisher and friends were perfectly willing to have this story voiced abroad as long as Fisher's name was withheld and his skin saved. Ultimately, the one fact that seemed worthy of contempt was that the good name of the community had been jeopardized by a few with petty, shallow and selfish concerns.

By early in the afternoon when Mrs. D'Ark called back to ask what was holding him up, L. had decided to reject the deal unless he was given without qualification the assurances he wanted. He found himself almost hoping the assurances would not be given, but he had nothing to worry about on that score. There would be no letter from Prentice-Hall, said Mrs. D'Ark. Her contact had said absolutely no letter of any kind. And no insured character references either. She had also received a clarification on a couple of other points. The reviews these people were talking about would appear in some of the smaller, "out-of-the-way" journals. ("They still don't want this book to get a lot of attention.") And the letters she would be able to write would not be exactly like those she had drafted to Wertham and Coles.

How would they differ? asked L.

Mrs. D'Ark explained that the other night her father had dropped by the house while she was working on the letter and, upon reading what she had written, had said, "Oh, no, you can't say it that way. You say it this way." And he had changed it to read not that she had come by her information directly from the source, but that she had simply heard people talking about what had been done to the book. She had changed it back to the truth in the letter she had already sent to Coles and in the one she was typing up right now for Wertham. But now the deal was that she could send only the kind of letter her father had approved.

"JoAnn," said L., "I think we'd better forget the whole thing."

"Why?" she asked.

L. reviewed all his reasons for rejecting the deal but dwelled on the one that had just surfaced. A letter, he explained, that said she had simply heard people talking about what had been done to the

121

book might be worse than no letter at all. For in that case she would be making a very serious charge on the basis of what would be considered hearsay or rumor, and there would be little or no chance to gain credibility. And as a result, the whole thing could backfire. She, and L. along with her, could be charged with spreading a scandalous story based on no more than gossip. And if she later tried to reverse herself and say, "Well, I didn't tell the truth the first time. I really got the story from the man responsible," who would believe her at that point?

"I didn't think of that," said Mrs. D'Ark.

"Well, this is the first thing that has made me kind of mad," said. L. "Because they're suggesting something here that could really get you into trouble. And me also. If you sent out letters like this, all they have to do is say, 'These people are using slanderous gossip in an effort to drum up the sales of the book.' And we come off looking terrible."

Mrs. D'Ark said she could understand L.'s reasons for not agreeing to the deal. It was true these people had not offered the slightest token of good faith and that he could not simply trust their word and wait for something nice to happen. Nonetheless, he felt there was some real disappointment in her voice. Her plan had been to resolve the matter quietly but equitably without anyone getting hurt. Now he was telling her it was not going to work.

Chapter 37

Their conversation was marked at this point by their one and only unpleasant exchange. Though its roots reached back to their first chat on the phone three and a half weeks earlier, it came seemingly without warning and reflected their disappointment and small unspoken suspicions.

Later L. would not recall exactly what he had said to trigger the response, but JoAnn D'Ark announced that there were a few things she had been meaning to say to him, things he wouldn't like to hear and she probably shouldn't say, but things she had to get off her chest. She had been disappointed in L. lately, she said, because she felt he was occasionally being hypocritical with her, and if there was one thing she could not stand, it was a person saying things he really didn't mean. At the beginning, she said, he had been full of compliments and flattery, but lately he seemed to have little concern for her, and now all of a sudden, all she had been hearing about was how he might get hurt this way or that way. He didn't really seem to care about her at all or about the trouble she had been letting herself in for. All he really seemed to care about was himself.

He knew that preliminary tests indicated that she might be faced again with a fatal disease, and yet he never asked about her health. And he hadn't told the truth, for example, when she had asked him to criticize her writing in the letter she had drafted to Wertham and Coles. He had made only a few suggestions and told her it was fine, but she had gone over it herself again and with his wife and had found a number of things that needed changing. It was obvious that he had not been honest about her writing, and she was afraid the same thing was going to happen in class with his wife. Getting a good and honest grade in her English course was very important to her. But she feared that with his wife as her teacher there would be no chance for a genuinely earned grade.

When she had finished, L. was aggressive in response. Look, he said, there was good reason for his "sudden" concern for his own welfare. Until now, they had really done little more than talk. They had written a few letters, made a few phone calls, but nothing of much consequence. Now, however, they had been forced to make a decision that could have a real impact; they were taking an action that could make a difference. And he simply wanted to make sure they were doing the right thing and that nobody, neither he nor she, got hurt. If she wrote those letters the way these people had dictated, they both might get hurt, and he was concerned about both of them.

As for compliments and expressions of concern, he had decided that she was not the kind of person who needed or even wanted that kind of reassurance on a regular basis, and he had assumed that she knew that he felt she was an extraordinary and remarkable person, worthy of considerable admiration, but that she would only be embarrassed by that kind of talk.

And finally with regard to her writing, she must understand that when he read the letter for her he was primarily concerned that it remain her own piece of work. He wanted to avoid imposing his style on something that should accurately reflect her own personality. Besides, he had been quite sure that she would see most of the needed changes for herself.

As for his wife, she was quite ruthless in going over someone else's work, including his own, and Mrs. D'Ark could be sure that she would earn whatever grade she finally got in his wife's course. Obviously, there were special circumstances here, and he and his wife had discussed the matter more than once. All he could say was that his wife was very aware of the problem and was determined to see that Mrs. D'Ark received an honest grade.

They had each spoken their piece, and L. felt the air had been cleared. It was time to move on to what they would do next. It was really L.'s move now, and they spent much of the afternoon considering the possibilities.

There were still a number of them, said L. After all, they still had reason to believe that Lou Gordon might take up the cause, and if he did, things might become very interesting. And then there were the letters they were sending to Wertham and Coles and their scheduled meeting with Bernard Rosenberg in a week or so. Something might come of these approaches. There was L.'s plan to go directly to Prentice-Hall and confront them with his information and then see what happened. And there was the plan suggested by his friend R. to send the whole story off to the people she knew at the New York Review of Books.

He explained R.'s idea in detail including the argument that the story could be presented in an effective and responsible way so that the blame would fall only where it should. The plan won JoAnn D'Ark's quick endorsement though not without some trepidation over the necessity of attaching her name to her story in public. She had said from the beginning that if this proved imperative to win justice for L. and his book, she was prepared to do it. Yet in the past few weeks she had been deeply disappointed by her failure to muster support for her effort and had sensed that she and her family might be ostracized by some of those she had been closest to ever since childhood. And certainly there was the possibility of a libel suit by Fisher or Prentice-Hall. If they carried through with a suit, considerable unpleasantness would result from their effort to discredit her as a reliable source.

Well, anyway, said Mrs. D'Ark, in case of a suit she could put whatever money and assets she had in her children's name. She had made her bed, and she would lie in it. She would write out her tale with Fisher's name included and sign it, but, she said, "Marv is going to kill me."

The husband was indeed troubled when he learned of the new developments later in the afternoon. On the phone with L. he wondered at how everything had changed so suddenly. First the plan had been for JoAnn to arrange a deal behind the scenes in which nobody got hurt, and now all of a sudden she was supposed to make her story public in a way that would force her into the center of a storm of controversy with all kinds of publicity and pressure. Again L. carefully explained his reasons for turning down the deal along with the arguments in favor of the plan to send the whole story to the New York Review of Books. Admittedly, said L., he had thought for a while that the best course for everyone involved was to keep the story from breaking over the community if at all possible. But lately he had begun to think that maybe the tale should be told, that perhaps making it public was the only proper thing to do. "I've been thinking," he said, "that what was done to this book is quite typical of much of what has been going on in this country, and that maybe it's important to expose this kind of thing when you have the chance.

Because maybe next time there won't be someone with the principled courage of a JoAnn D'Ark to stand up and act on their conscience. Maybe if we make the effort this time, next time somebody will think twice about doing something like this."

Marv seemed torn between his desire to see justice done and his natural and quite sensible concern for the welfare of his wife and family. He understood L.'s position, he said, but he just couldn't let JoAnn subject herself to the pressures that would inevitably follow if she publicly attached her name to her charges. He was deeply concerned about JoAnn's health and really didn't think she should be involved in such things, at least until they had a definite indication of her condition. Under the circumstances he couldn't allow JoAnn to sign a statement naming Fisher. Besides, L. himself had said there were other possible routes that did not necessarily involve JoAnn making a target of herself. Why not at least wait to see their outcome?

L. was disappointed but saw no way to argue with Marv's position. Instead, he asked if they'd give him a chance to make a copy of the letter JoAnn was about to mail to Fredric Wertham. This told the story without naming Fisher, and L. could go to Prentice-Hall, confront them with the letter, but keep its author anonymous. Marv said he had no problem with this plan and in fact personally delivered the letter to L.'s home early the following afternoon. L. read through it carefully and was pleased and relieved to have something tangible in his hands. Mrs. D'Ark's neat, single-spaced typing covered three pages of her personally inscribed stationery and ended with her signature. He took the letter to a local library with a copying machine, made three copies, then slipped it into its envelope addressed to Wertham's home in Pennsylvania and dropped it in a mailbox.

Chapter 38

On the following Sunday morning, according to his weekly custom, L. drove to Dexter-Davidson to buy bagels. Less than a mile from his home, the shopping plaza was a small collection of Jewish stores, including a delicatessen, a book and gift shop, the beautifully stocked supermarket that gave the plaza its name, and a bagel factory that sold hot fresh bagels by the hundreds.

It was always a bustling, fascinating place on Sunday, and after years of weekly visits L. felt something there akin to a sense of community even though he rarely met anyone he knew.

There was always someone to exchange a few words with—the B'nai B'rith kids hawking their bake sale goods or raffle tickets; politicians shaking hands and passing out literature; a matron with a can collecting for Jewish orphans; the little old balloon man who was not happy if L. said, "Keep the change," when he bought his son a fifteen cent "Swissy Mouse" balloon and paid for it with a quarter; and the young Hasidim with their fedoras and beards who wanted to convince him to use the tefillin or to usher his son into the "Sukkahmobile" parked in front of the bagel factory, its loudspeaker' blaring happy Hasidic music. L. was always amused and embarrassed by their embarrassment when he had to tell them he wasn't Jewish--he looked Jewish, everybody said.

Everywhere in the market greetings were exchanged and conversations struck up. "Where old friends meet to shop and save" was the store's motto. L. was always intrigued by its collection of shoppers: teenagers in baseball uniforms and yarmulkes and old men with their late morning cigars; neatly dressed rabbis with skeptical eyes and bored, cynical-looking academics with beautiful children; slim, attractive young mothers pushing bulging shopping carts and house-dressed housewives sampling the grapes; lawyers, judges, and doctors unshaven and casually dressed and businessmen in shag haircuts, mod knits and boots; an aristocratic, goateed old psychoanalyst, a pair of long-haired young lovers checking items on the commune's shopping list and the occasional survivor with a heavy European accent, numbers tattooed on the wrist and a 30-year-old horror still haunting dark eyes.

On this particular Sunday, with company coming, L. bought two packages of cream cheese instead of one, twice as many bagels as usual, some butterhorns and cinnamon pastries.

At one o'clock people began to arrive at L.'s little bungalow, first R. and her husband, then Bernard Rosenberg and the old friend he was staying with in Detroit, and finally JoAnn D'Ark.

L. had spoken briefly with Rosenberg the night before on the phone but had muffed his chance to confess that Mrs. D'Ark's call to Chicago had not come simply on her own initiative, but rather at L.'s suggestion. He was anxious to correct this last bit of deception, but Rosenberg, had seemed a little skeptical and had said half-seriously that he hoped he hadn't stuck L. with a crazy woman by encouraging Mrs. D'Ark to get in touch with him. L. had said only that after a thorough investigation he had found no reason to disbelieve the woman. Now thinking Mrs. D'Ark would be embarrassed by the story, he decided he would have to make his confession at some later date and ask forgiveness.

With everyone in L.'s small living room munching baked goods, drinking coffee, and smoking cigarettes, pipes, and cigars, Rosenberg's courteous skepticism set the conversational tone. It was a common occurrence, said the small, dark sociologist with a reputation for keen insight and quick wit, for a publisher to provide little or no support for a book, to toss it on the market and leave it for dead. Unfortunately it was all part of the business, and the industry's history was filled with sad examples of good books abandoned by their careless or uncaring publishers. His own most recent book had quickly sold out its ten thousand copy first printing, and now the company had decided against another printing run; in effect it was already out of print.

Finally, Mrs. D'Ark spoke up, saying with emotion that she felt that some of those present had apparently decided that she wasn't telling the truth.

Rosenberg said kindly that this wasn't the case at all. No one was saying that she hadn't told the truth about what she had heard from this man, whoever he was. It was just that a more credible explanation for what she had heard was that the man had perhaps been boasting or had elaborated on the facts to make himself look important. When Rosenberg's friend echoed his skepticism and guessed wrongly at the name of the man responsible, L. decided it was time for an announcement.

"Look," he said, "there's no reason not to use the name of the man we've been talking about. It's Max Fisher."

There was a pause during which L. could feel the room's atmosphere changing. Rosenberg's friend, a long-time resident of Detroit's Jewish community and personally acquainted with Fisher, said, "Oh, well, that's a different story! Now this is getting interesting. Max is capable of wanting to do something like this and capable of doing it."

The next several minutes were devoted to a discussion of the power, position, where-with-all and inclinations of Max Fisher, mostly for the benefit of Rosenberg, who had no knowledge of the man. R.'s husband explained that during the period when the approach must have been made to Prentice-Hall (late 1969 or early 1970), New Detroit, Inc., with Fisher as chairman, had authorized several thousands of dollars for the purchase of textbooks for Detroit schools. When it was added finally that Fisher had close ties with the current administration, Rosenberg turned a sad smile to L. and asked, "How long do you think it will take you to become anti-Semitic?"

L. laughed easily, grateful for the trust. Later in taking leave, Rosenberg said he would ask about the book among his friends in New York, where he would visit soon, and would suggest it for review to a respected Jewish journal. Before the gathering broke up, however, L. asked Mrs. D'Ark to repeat a story she had told him earlier in the week after the deal had been offered.

Apparently word of her approach to L. had made the rounds, she said, because she had received a phone call from an old man who was a family friend she had known most of her life.

"Well, the first thing he said was, 'I always thought you had a big mouth.' And when I asked him what he meant, he said, 'What I want to know is why a young, inexperienced, immature person like you decided to take it on yourself to *reverse an injustice*, when there were men in the community much older and wiser and more experienced than you, who had decided that this was something that was necessary?'

"And I. said, 'Well, of course, I know that I'm young and in-experienced and immature and that these men are older and wiser' and more experienced than I am. And that's why I decided to go for advice to some other men who are even older and even wiser. And if you'd like to know what they told me, I'll go get the Talmud and read it to you.'

"And he just started sputtering in Yiddish and saying things like, 'I always knew you were a smart-ass.'"

Chapter 39

One sunny autumn afternoon in the year they were both seventeen, L. had caught a football thrown eighty yards in the air by his friend Dave DeBusschere. They had just been whiling away time after school, kicking and tossing the ball around a practice field. But the catch had always highlighted L.'s secret reveries as a frustrated sports hero. Now as he stood with his father in the famed Manhattan bookstore Brentano's leafing through DeBusschere's new book, a diary of the New York Knicks' championship season called *The Open Man*, he was thinking of irony again.

As a 16-year-old community newspaper reporter writing about DeBusschere's athletic exploits every week, he had first learned the pleasures of constructing a well-made sentence. He had known then that his friend was destined for extraordinary acclaim as an athlete; he had not guessed that Dave would also become an author in the same fall that would see his own first book published. The excerpts he had read in New York magazine had shown DeBusschere's good, wry sense of humor, and the book had reportedly sold 25,000 copies.

To their surprise L. and his father found two copies of *Murder in the Synagogue* in Brentano's — shelved with the store's religious books. More predictably the clerks at Scribner's and Doubleday's had never heard of the book.

It was Wednesday, March 24, and earlier in the day L.'s father had paid another call to the Amalgamated Building on Union Square. Now they walked to their afternoon appointment at the offices of the literary agent Julian Bach. L. had arranged the meeting a week earlier on the phone and recalled how distant Bach's voice had become when L. explained why he was coming to New York. "I must really sound paranoid," he had told himself after hanging up.

Judging by the many familiar books and dust jackets displayed in his waiting room, Mr. Bach was a busy and successful agent. They began the meeting in the man's large, high-ceilinged office with L.

asking Bach to read the two page factual summary he had prepared. It was essentially the same thing he had sent to Lou Gordon, although he had added a paragraph about his experience with his former agent, the erstwhile Jules Fields:

"One last note: when I received the final $4000 of my advance in March 1970, I was urged by Prentice-Hall to formally sever connections with my agent, Mr. Fields. I did so, since Mr. Fields had for some time not responded to my inquiries and since P-H told me that Mr. Fields was more or less out of the business and that they had had some difficulty in getting checks through him to authors. Recently I was told by the writer who originally led me to Fields that he is still very much in the business and gives her the impression that he's still my agent. Of course, if this were so, he would be currently eschewing the $400 rightfully his as a 10% cut of the remainder of my advance."

Bach's first reaction was to announce that he was certainly not about to advise them to "sue the hell out of Prentice-Hall." That was a decision for a lawyer to make, and he wanted no part of any such action. In fact, though he had previously said he would handle the sale of the book's subsidiary rights, he now made it clear that while he was still interested in seeing L.'s future work, he would have nothing to do with this book. With this point established and with an assurance from L.'s father that they had no legal action in mind and had only come to him for whatever friendly advice he could offer, Bach proceeded to comment on what L. had given him to read.

The $8500 advance secured by Jules Fields, he said, was an extraordinary sum for Prentice-Hall to give an untried author. He didn't know Mr. Fields but felt the agent had done a remarkable job in getting that much from a company that just didn't toss that kind of money around. "I doubt if I could have done it," he said and added that they must have had high hopes for the book.

The editorial problems with the manuscript, said Bach, were L.'s fault. It was simply unprofessional to deliver a 1000 page script to your publisher. The book, however, had definitely been overpriced: $9.95 was a "ridiculous" price for the book." And it had been thoroughly unprofessional of the people at Prentice-Hall to in effect slander Jules Fields to L. This kind of thing just wasn't done. On the other hand, said Bach upon hearing of L.'s experience with Fields in Central Park, it was unprofessional of an agent to take more than his

10 percent.

As for the rest of the details, the agent admitted that it looked like L. might well have been victimized, and he vowed that as a Jew he personally found the idea of such an action against the book to be obnoxious. Nonetheless, his advice in this case, to a young writer with a good solid book already under his belt and his whole career ahead of him, was quite frankly to avoid raising an uproar and causing a lot of trouble. Go to Prentice-Hall, he suggested, tell them that you've been upset by this story you've heard in Detroit, and ask perhaps for a list of those who were sent review copies if you think there was a problem in that area. But don't go in hurling charges and making threats, because they're not going to get you anywhere. And when you've had your say, then your best possible course would be to simply drop the subject, chalk it up as an unfortunate experience, forget about it, and get on to something else.

Julian Bach leaned back and peered at them through his mod-styled horn rims. He seemed a man of some taste and no little sophistication. But L. had been irked at one point with the condescending way Bach had explained that while L. was a young writer of some talent, it was also clear that he was not destined to join the ranks of the world's great novelists—a gratuitous remark, L. thought, meant to encourage a humble acceptance of the advice being offered.

"If you don't let the matter rest," said Bach, "and instead persist in giving Prentice-Hall a hard time and in the process gain the reputation of being a trouble-maker, you're certainly not going to do yourself or your book any good. You'll only be jeopardizing your chances in the future."

He gestured vaguely at his windows overlooking 48th Street. "Look, this twenty square block area of Manhattan is the American publishing establishment. And they've all had their experiences like this. They'll understand Prentice-Hall's position in this thing, and they'll close ranks and pull together, and you may never get another book published."

They talked for a while longer, and L. said he was going to ask the company for an immediate reversion of rights. Bach said he didn't think Prentice-Hall would agree. "It would set a precedent they wouldn't want to set."

Finally, the agent, glancing at his watch, announced that he'd given them an hour of his time mainly because he felt that what had happened to L. and his book was unfortunate and because he would hate to see L. jeopardize his career by doing something now that was ill-advised.

L. left promising to send Bach some of his short stories and to report the outcome of his visit to Prentice-Hall. Privately he doubted that he would do either. Afterward in a nearby bar he sipped a Scotch and told his father why he was not about to take what he felt had been somewhat self-serving advice from Bach.

"He knows we're going to talk to Prentice-Hall tomorrow, and he doesn't want us going over there and saying, 'Look, I talked with my agent Julian Bach yesterday, and he says such and such, that you should have done this or that.' After all I got his name from Mossman at Prentice-Hall, which probably means that he frequently does business over there. And if he does, he certainly doesn't want me going there and causing trouble and telling them that he's my agent and that I'm acting on his advice. That's why I have to take with a grain of salt what he says about jeopardizing my career and all that crap about the 'American publishing establishment.' I mean there are a lot of publishers in this country, and they're not all in this 'twenty-square block area of Manhattan.' If you write a good book, sooner or later you'll find somebody to publish it. Maybe he's right about the big houses in the establishment, maybe they will act that way, but there are other places that don't necessarily have the same concerns.

"All I'm saying is that it seems to me that Bach is telling me to go easy and not cause trouble primarily out of a concern for his own situation with Prentice-Hall."

L. was speaking earnestly but had not thought carefully about what he was saying. He could tell that his father had been impressed and worried by Bach's advice, the effect of which L. was trying to counter. Still, he now found himself agreeing that it might be smarter to start off quietly with Prentice-Hall, to test the waters first before plunging in with accusations and threats. Before their talk with Bach. L.'s plan was to approach Prentice-Hall with guns drawn, their outrage showing, and with threats and even a bluff if necessary. Now he told himself they could toughen their posture at any time after they got a look at the company's position.

Chapter 40

From the bar shortly before five, L.'s father finally made a tentatively successful phone call to Prentice-Hall. For a week he had tried and failed to reach the firm's president, a man named Frank Dunnigan, but this time a vice-president in charge of public relations said that, though everyone had gone home for the day, he would leave word for the president of the trade division, Wilber Eastman, to expect a call in the morning and to set aside some time tomorrow for a meeting. Feeling that Fisher had probably approached the man at the top, L. had wanted to confront Mr. Dunnigan. The man on the phone, however, said Dunnigan would not be available and that Eastman would be the one to speak to about the book anyway. L.'s father had said only that they had come from Detroit to bring an urgent matter concerning the book to the company's attention.

After dinner at a nearby Italian restaurant, L. dragged his father down to Madison Square Garden where their alma mater was playing in the second round of the N.I.T. L. had retained enough of his boyhood passion for sports to use an occasional basketball game as an effective narcotic, which was what he wanted on this particular night in Manhattan. Michigan played badly and lost, but the game served the purpose. Afterward they drove their rented car across the George Washington Bridge and found a room at a Holiday Inn just outside Englewood Cliffs.

In the morning after breakfast, L.'s father placed his call to Eastman. As usual L. envied his father's cordial ease on the phone.

"No, I don't think that'll be necessary," he was saying. Eastman had asked if he should bring one of the firm's attorneys along to the meeting. "This is something we felt we should bring to your attention before going any further with it, and quite frankly we think you'll be grateful to us for doing so."

L. wondered if they were hitting Mr. Eastman cold or if he had been warned by someone in Detroit. At first he had thought it likely that Fisher or one of his people had sounded the alarm immediately and that the company would be on red alert. Later he had come to doubt that anyone had made such an embarrassing phone call—it was probably every man for himself now.

Besides, the company had probably covered its tracks well enough that they wouldn't even need a warning. Whatever the case, L. felt Eastman's question about bringing along an attorney suggested that the trade division president had a good idea of what they had come to talk about.

The meeting was scheduled for noon. During the morning they settled their strategy, with L. agreeing to let his father tell the story and do their talking at the start. Later they visited the little park on the cliffs over the Hudson. Bright clear spring sunlight surprised L. with a fine view of the New York skyline. The light of truth has burned away the murky haze of falsehood, he joked to himself. He was in a good mood, calm and alert. Unlike the day before when he had been tense and preoccupied before meeting with Bach.

They waited for Eastman in the reception lounge at Prentice Hall, and after several minutes the man appeared: dark suit and dark-rimmed glasses, medium build and closer to L.'s 6'2" than his father's 5'8", late forties or early fifties, L. guessed, face in a serious cast but a brief smile for L. and his father as they shook hands, a poised and cordial manner. The man's composure was in fact complete except for the unfortunate tic, which L. quickly noted in the left side of the face, a small and occasional spasm that closed the left eye for an unmistakable split-second.

In all, at first glance, almost a model of the upper echelon bureaucrat, blending almost invisibly with the landscape of the organization, yet set apart from his fellows by the necessity of making decisions for which he might be called to account, the pressure nearly mastered but not quite, the failure focused in that telling twitch, the sad, involuntary wink.

Eastman said he thought they might do their talking over lunch and had sent his director of publicity, Nick D'Incecco, to bring a car around for the drive to a nearby restaurant. Moments later L. and his father were introduced to D'Incecco, a friendly, open-faced man in his late thirties, and settled themselves in the back seat of the car. From the front Eastman kept a casual conversation going with L.'s father by asking small-talk questions phrased in a way that L. found amusing.

"You work in corporation law in Detroit?"

"That's right. I specialize in labor relations..."

And a minute or two later: "And you have another son who works in your firm?"

"Yes, Vince's been with me for almost two years now..."

Sounds like they've been doing a little quick research, L. thought to himself. On the phone his father had simply identified himself as an attorney, saying nothing about his practice.

Within a few minutes they were inside Sid Allen's, a softly lit, well-appointed restaurant, checking their overcoats. L. had decided his conservative tweed was more appropriate for this trip. Also checked was the attache case he had carried in. He caught Eastman eying it for a second, wondering, perhaps, what L. was planning to spring at him from its secret interior. In fact, since it contained little more than a copy of Mrs. D'Ark's letter, which L. and his father had decided not to show Eastman anyway, he had brought the case along mostly for its visual effect.

At their table L. sat across from D'Incecco with Eastman on the right and his father on the left. They all ordered drinks except D'Incecco, who refrained for a reason L. didn't catch. Eastman had his usual, a large Manhattan, the size of which he joked about in advance; the way they made them at this place, it would only *appear* larger than normal.

The amiable small talk continued for a while with L. still on the sidelines: he hadn't spoken except for their introductions. How were business conditions in Detroit? Not good. The latest word was that the auto companies had decided to forego styling changes until 1975 in an effort to keep costs down while adding the new government-required safety features. As a result the tool and dye people were going to be hurting badly.

Was industry really concerned about the environment or was it only spending heavily on advertising to make the public think so? The concern was genuine, but with business down there were some difficult choices to make. The real problem with the economy was the administration's failure to enact wage and price controls when it should have done so some months back. This last point from his Nixonite father surprised L.

They ordered their food and then finally got down to business. L.'s father began by emphasizing that they were neophytes. When the book was published, they had been hopeful, of course, but not quite sure what to expect. Subsequently, they had been disappointed at the book's lack of success and puzzled along the way at some of the things Prentice-Hall had done with the book. They had wondered about these things, he said, but had decided that the publisher certainly knew its business better than they did, and so they would simply rely on its judgment.

Then just a few weeks back, a young woman had come to them completely on her own initiative with a story that frankly, upon first hearing, they had found difficult to believe. This was a woman from a fine family in Detroit with no apparent reason to tell them anything but the truth, and she was saying that she had heard a man with one of the most prominent names in the city say that he had suppressed this book.

L. had been listening with some impatience to his father's rather sketchy presentation and finally decided that he should be telling the tale himself. He found an opening to suggest that he might take over effectively, and his father relinquished the floor without hesitation. As Eastman and D'Incecco turned their eyes to him, it was obvious that he had an engrossed audience.

L. built his case slowly, emphasizing the care with which he had investigated this woman and her story, listing the facts of her background and quoting the words of the rabbi "in a prominent position in the city" who had vouched for her integrity and honesty. He explained when and how she had come by her information and then carefully detailed the facts of her story just as she had recited them. Eastman was silent throughout and L. concluded:

"The important point is that, according to this woman's story, she is not repeating hearsay or rumor, and she's talking about a man with the kind of power and influence required to do something like this. She says she got her information directly from the man who claimed responsibility. And Max Fisher" — L. paused just slightly and carefully watched Eastman's face — "is not a man who makes idle boasts."

Until this point L. had avoided using Fisher's name, and now in that slim pause after its invocation, Eastman's left eye had snapped shut and then opened again in a wink that had seemed almost confirmation.

Chapter 41

L. found Eastman's initial comments, however, quite resourceful. Instead of denying any knowledge of someone named Max Fisher, he immediately admitted a certain acquaintance and described his "one experience" with the man. A few years back, he explained, Prentice-Hall had published a political biography of George Romney. And while the book was being prepared—this was at a time when Romney was a leading contender for the Republican nomination—Max Fisher had placed an order with the company for 10,000 copies. Then sometime later, on the day, in fact, established as the book's publication date, Romney had announced in New Hampshire his withdrawal from the race.

"And the following day," said Eastman with a slight grin, "Max Fisher called me and cancelled his order." This was the extent of his acquaintance with Mr. Fisher, and he had never encountered the man again.

Sounding amiable and conciliatory, L.'s father explained that they were, of course, making no charges and planned no legal action at this time, but they had been disturbed and puzzled by this story, and they wanted to give the company a chance to hear the details and to react to them. They felt Prentice-Hall deserved this chance before anything else might be done, and they hoped the company understood the friendly spirit with which it was given.

Oh, absolutely, said Eastman, Prentice-Hall was very grateful to L. and his father for handling the matter in this way and for bringing this information to the company's attention. If Max Fisher had the kind of power and connections necessary to reach various newspapers and magazines around the country and keep them from giving this book reviews or publicity, then Prentice-Hall certainly wanted to know about it and greatly appreciated the effort to bring this information to them. After all, if Fisher could do this to L.'s book, he might take it into his head to do the same thing to other Prentice-

Hall books in the future. And this was certainly something they would have to consider carefully.

L. was highly amused at the turn Eastman's line had taken. After L. had clearly established that his charge involve Prentice-Hall's collusion with Mr. Fisher, and after Eastman himself had tacitly acknowledged this with his anecdote about the Romney book, the trade division president was suddenly trying to ally his firm with L. in the role of Mr. Fisher's victim.

The ploy was to play "Everybody against Max Fisher," mused L. to himself. But later he would wonder why a man as intelligent as Eastman would try something so transparent. Perhaps, he would speculate later, Eastman had misread his father's conciliatory remarks as an opening to an "understanding" that L. wanted to reach with Prentice-Hall. But that was not what L. was looking for.

Instead he reminded Eastman and D'Incecco that the import of his informant's story, as he was sure he had made clear in the first place, was that Fisher had said flatly that he had been promised by the *publisher* that certain things would be done to "squelch" the book.

D'Incecco spoke first with a look of shocked incredulity: "He said the publisher had promised to do this?"

"That's right," said L., and he stopped further reaction for the moment by adding, "But there's a bit more to this story which I think you should probably know about." With Eastman's rather grim nod, he quickly covered the last piece of Mrs. D'Ark's tale, the offer of a deal from Fisher and those involved with him.

When he had finished, he paused briefly, noting a certain gloom over the table, and then explained: "My problem now is what to do with this story. I've spent the last month or so trying very hard to find some reason to disbelieve what this woman told me, both in terms of her character and background and in terms of the facts of the publishing history of my book—just what Prentice-Hall did or didn't do with reference to it. And frankly I haven't been able to come up with a single reason. Yesterday we talked with a top agent in New York who advised me not to cause trouble when I came to meet you today, because he said 'this twenty square block area of Manhattan is the publishing establishment, and they've all had their experiences like this.' So I take it that this kind of thing happens occasionally."

As might be expected, Eastman quickly set out to solve L.'s

problem. He could assure L. and his father right now, he said, that there just wasn't any truth to this story. He had personally set the price of the book, just as he set the prices of all the books on their list. And there were many factors to be considered in each decision. As for reviews, there was just no way Prentice-Hall could affect whether their books were reviewed or not. All they could do was send out review copies and hope for the best. In fact, if they tried to intercede for a book in some way, the effort would probably backfire. Originally they had entertained high hopes for L.'s book as indicated by the size of the advance they had given him. And by the way, said Eastman, even though the company might lose money on a book, it was not their policy to ask an author to repay the advance he had been given.

How nice, thought L.

Eastman explained that they had first thought in terms of a possible sale of 20,000 for L.'s book, but unfortunately, for some reason it simply hadn't generated that much interest.

As a matter of fact, said L., the book had received some excellent comments from a number of prominent people and in several out-of-the-way reviews. He imagined they were aware of these, he said and pulled from a pocket of his corduroy sport coat copies of his ads with the quotes from Drs. Wertham and Coles, Professor Shneidman, and Rabbis Riemer and Mandel.

Eastman and D'Incecco read intently, as if they hadn't seen the comments before, and L. explained the background of the ads: how Prentice-Hall had failed to use the quote from Wertham in its few useless ads; how L. and his father had been forced to pay the full cost of their ads after Miller in advertising had reneged on his promise to cover half the cost (Eastman quickly assured them the company would make good its promise); and how in effect Prentice-Hall had passed up every chance to let people know that the book had won praise.

From advertising L. moved to the "blunders" of the publicity department, explaining the Morning Show mix-up and the likelihood that he had missed other shows in Detroit because Miss Neger had not told him of Bob Yoder's arrangements. Moreover, the book editor of the Detroit News and TV commentator Lou Gordon had both denied having heard of the book. By the time L. got to Miss Neger's failure to send author's request copies to several important people and tossed in the fact that a number of stores in Detroit had been unable to get the book on reorder for several weeks during the fall, Eastman was resorting to sympathy and understanding.

"Yes," he said. "I can certainly see how you must have been disturbed and upset by all of this. There was a pattern in all of it. Everything seemed to fit a pattern!"

At one point, when D'Incecco began to explain Pat Neger's consistent failure to answer L.'s letters and calls by saying that she had been very busy, Eastman cut him off abruptly: "No, that's no excuse. There's no excuse for that kind of thing, and I can tell you she'll hear about it."

One answer he never had been able to get, said L., though he had asked everyone he had spoken to at Prentice-Hall, was the size of the book's first printing. D'Incecco said he wasn't sure but thought it was either 4000, 5000 or 6000.

"You mean you really don't know?" asked L. "I really find it very strange that no one at Prentice-Hall can tell me how many copies of my book were printed. Who makes that decision?"

"I do," admitted Eastman. "And it was either 4-or-5000. I don't recall exactly. But that's one answer we can get for you right away. As soon as we get back to the office, I'll look that up for you."

L. was already sure it was 4000, a number he associated with sure-flop first novels. His father asked if it was possible that an approach from Detroit had been made to Prentice-Hall and perhaps something done without Eastman or D'Incecco knowing about it.

Well, of course, he was hearing about all of this for the first time today, said Eastman, so he couldn't speak for others at Prentice-Hall and say flatly that no one else had been approached. D'Incecco, as he had before, was shaking his head and saying the whole thing was incredible. "So many people would have had to have been involved in so many departments, that it's just impossible for us not to have known if something had been done."

Later L. would think carefully about this point and decide that Eastman would have kept the number at a bare minimum. He claimed to have made all the crucial decision himself on price, print run, etc., and perhaps all he would have had to tell people like Mossman, Neger, and possibly even the heads of advertising and in subsidiary rights was that the company had given up on the book. Even D'Incecco could have been honestly ignorant.

Eastman asked casually now if this woman who had come to L. knew or perhaps could find out from these people in Detroit the name of the person at Prentice-Hall Fisher had actually contacted.

An interesting question, thought L., and, smugly pleased with the conversation so far, he simply told the truth rather than use the con that would keep Eastman properly worried. No, the jig was up in Detroit, he said, and these people knew this woman had come to him. They were not about to give her any further information. Frankly, he said, he felt Fisher had probably gone to someone at the top of the firm, and he implied that Eastman and his trade division probably weren't important enough to rate a call from Max.

Finally, L. decided to make his case in terms that would be easy for Eastman to undermine if the firm had nothing to hide. He really didn't see how this thing could have been done, he said, if all of the review copies had been sent to those who should have received them. For once a book got into the hands of the important reviewers, its fate was no longer under the total control of its publisher. In other words, he was suggesting that the company had sent out something less than a full compliment of review copies. And so he was asking Eastman for two things: 1) some kind of credible evidence that a full compliment had indeed gone out, and 2) a promise that L. would receive a complete list of those to whom the books had been sent.

Eastman offered neither. Instead he talked in generalities about the promotion Prentice-Hall did for each of its books (300 review copies, etc.) and asked D'Incecco to check on a possible slip up with the Detroit papers in this case. And finally, he confided to L. that even if the important New York reviewers did not receive review copies of a particular book, it did not necessarily mean the book was dead. Nearly every book was treated in two or three preview-reviews, and these alone could spark enough interest to get a book moving.

"Yeah," said L. with a smile, "that's the only thing I haven't been able to explain in all of this. Of all the reviews and comments the book got, the only ones with a negative tone were those three preview reviews. I'd really like to know how that was done."

Chapter 42

They talked for a while about subsidiary rights, Eastman explaining that earlier in the morning after receiving their call he had asked D'Incecco to go over their records on the book.

Getting the book into paperback and thus making it available at a decent price was still his major concern, said L., but he had been told there were no takers. That was right, said D'Incecco, though there had been expressions of interest in other areas. Like what? asked L. Well, for example, the Commentary Library had shown some interest in the book though they had finally decided against it.

"I'm sorry," said L., his voice with an edge in it for the first time, "but that's not quite accurate as I understand it. John Nelson told me back in November that the Commentary Library had definitely wanted the book, but that Prentice-Hall had refused to sell it to them for the price offered."

D'Incecco admitted that he didn't have all the facts. Eastman said he thought it might be a good idea for the company to make another effort to sell the book to a paperback house and perhaps go back to the Commentary Library and see if they could still work out a deal. After all Prentice-Hall would like a chance to get some of its money back on this book.

L. said it seemed a little strange that now all of a sudden they were interested in doing something for the book. They had, of course, known for some time about the praise the book had received and about the offer from the Commentary people. He didn't understand why they were only now getting interested.

"It sounds," said D' Incecco with a puzzled look, "like you don't want us to do these things."

And L. replied, "Well, frankly, no, I don't. I'm sure you can understand how my trust and confidence in the company have been undermined by this story. And what I really want is simply to have my book back, to have the rights reverted to me as soon as possible."

Eastman said this would have to be discussed with others in the firm and wondered if it would be all right if he got back to L.'s father with their answer in a week and a half.

Fine, said his father, who then launched into a friendly, fatherly discussion of how much time and effort his son had put into this book and how understandable it was that the young man should be upset by what had happened. "And, of course, I ask myself, 'What can I do to make this young fellow happy again.'"

It seemed to L. that his father's very affability carried a menacing quality now, that even those smiling disclaimers of plans for legal action contained their threat. He excused himself and walked to the men's room. Washing his hands, he glanced up at the mirror and found his face slightly flushed and obviously pleased. After 90 minutes of talk, he had raised every one of his points, and the gentlemen from Prentice-Hall had managed few if any reasonable answers. Was there anything else he wanted to say? Ah, yes, he had one more thing in mind.

As he arrived back at their table, his father was saying for the third (and last) time that they had no plans at this point to take legal action.

"You know," said L. seating himself, "My father is a lawyer, and he thinks in legal terms. I'm a writer, and I think in somewhat different terms. I've spent a great deal of time and energy, first in working on this book and then in tracking done and sorting out the story of what happened to it. Quite frankly, I'm sick of the whole business and I'd like nothing better than to put it all behind me and get on to something else. Yet at the same time I must say it's been a fascinating experience, and I'm sure it would make a fascinating story."

The longest, most awkward silence of the afternoon followed, until L.'s father finally delivered a kind of verbal slap on the wrist: "Now, Tom, we don't want to talk that way..."

By now they were all pushing their chairs back and getting to their feet. Their luncheon discussion was over, and L. led the way to the checkroom. Outside the sun was shining as brightly as ever, and the small talk resumed on their way back to the company offices. "Your crocuses are up; ours haven't made it yet," said L. as they walked past neatly edged beds at the entrance to the editorial offices.

Eastman said he was pressed for time and left L. and his father in

D'Incecco's hands after promising to get them the information about the first printing size before they left. A few minutes later he reappeared just long enough to say, "It was 4000."

They were sitting around a large table in a small glass-walled meeting room with D'Incecco shuffling through a couple of files on the book. L. had a brief look at the forms Bob Yoder had filled out with details of three appearances he had set up on Detroit-area shows. Apparently he had added one after they had spoken on the phone, and he had put them all in writing for Miss Neger. L. declined to glance through a pile of small blue slips, each with the name and address of someone who had supposedly been sent a review copy. He wanted not a quick look but a complete list, which he would ask for at a later date and he found the three new reviews from Dallas, Kansas City, and Allentown.

D'Incecco provided them with the last two copies of the book in the office, and L.'s father, leafing through one of them with his still-amiable smile, said, "You people certainly couldn't have expected to sell many copies of this book at $9.95."

And D'Incecco—not really hearing those words or bedazzled by that smile—agreed.

PART IV

Chapter 43

In the week after his return from New York L. received letters from Drs. Wertham and Coles, each offering encouragement and advice and a promise to talk with others about the book. Apparently Mrs. D'Ark's letter had made a good impression: she too received a heartening response from each psychiatrist.

The story, wrote Wertham, "sounds very likely. Publishers are very sensitive to any such suggestions." Coles advised that L. get in touch with a good investigative reporter, and Wertham had a word of warning about L.'s hope to get the book into paperback. He would welcome such a development, he said, but L. should know that "a very severe form of censorship" can be exercised by the large distributors in the paperback end of the publishing world. If distributors covering a substantial market area refused to handle a particular book, its chances of ever issuing in paperback were not very good. L. wrote back promptly to each man, describing in detail the events of the past two weeks. His letters reflected the good spirits he had returned with from New York He felt that both Eastman and D'Incecco had more than once tipped their hands and had failed to provide him with any reason to disbelieve Mrs. D'Ark's story.

Influenced by Julian Bach, he now guessed that Prentice-Hall would not want to return the book's rights, at least for a while, and would instead try to mollify him by announcing a paperback offer. He doubted there was anything more to fear from Fisher. It now seemed to be every man for himself, and Max would probably not be interested in having anything further to do with the book.

In a way L. was almost hoping against a paperback offer through the company, because if one did come, he would probably have to take it and thus recommit himself to Prentice-Hall instead of making a clean break. Despite Wertham's warning, he was confident he could sell the paperback rights himself once he owned the book again. As for Coles' suggestion of an investigative reporter, L. still held out mild hope that Lou Gordon might take up the cause. Gordon, of course, billed himself as the most fearless reporter in town, beholden to no one, frequently reporting stories that neither of Detroit's newspapers would touch. It had only been two weeks since they had talked on the phone, and L. thought it likely that Gordon would at least call Mrs. D'Ark to check out her full story.

At the moment Mrs. D'Ark was amused with the fact that Fisher and those who had made the offer of a deal were apparently under the impression that L. had humbly and gratefully accepted its terms. At the time, she had passed along L.'s initial reaction ("Sounds good.") and had perhaps mitigated his demands for assurances with her own eagerness to see the deal accepted and the matter settled.

These people had been so sure that L. had no alternative, she said, that they had just assumed, with no further word from her, his agreement. Her father, who L. was sure had served as a go-between, had hinted that she should hurry if she had something to tell him, because he would be away on business for a while. But Mrs. D'Ark never again raised the subject, nor did her father.

On Monday, April 5th, exactly a week and a half after their meeting in Englewood Cliffs, L.'s father received a letter from Eastman. It proposed that the company immediately declare the book out of print and revert all rights to the author—on condition that L. and his father immediately purchase the remaining 1400 copy inventory of the book at the unit manufacturing cost of $2.25 per copy.

L. was more than a little perturbed with the idea that they would have to pay thousands of dollars and store hundreds of books in order to get the rights back. He quickly drafted a reply that talked tough and raised the ante; he thought the time had come to stiffen their posture. His father, however, felt they would get farther by remaining cordial and avoiding threats. Only later would L. understand his father's unstated logic—that the company would be less willing to give them what they wanted, if in doing so it would appear to be acting under the pressure of their threats. If their talk got too tough, the company might simply refer the matter to its attorneys and refuse to move at all. For the better part of a week L. and his father argued over the alternatives, until they finally decided on a compromise in which his father would draft the letter but close with a sentence that L. had concocted to sound menacing but say little:

> In reviewing your proposal, it seems to me that the requirement that we purchase from you the remaining copies of the book and any future returns is somewhat inequitable. Your company is in a much better position to dispose of these books through normal channels, and I believe that some extra effort or incentive at a lower price would make this possible. We, on the other hand, have no such sources available to us.
>
> The remaining items would be acceptable if you included the transfer of the plates for the book, which would be of no further value to you.
>
> Frankly, accumulating evidence of the truth of the story we brought to you has convinced us that our proposal deserves your careful consideration.

Securing the plates on which the book had been printed was an idea that L. had harbored for some time. If they could be acquired, thus reducing future production costs to a minimum, L. had felt there might even be a chance to find a house interested in reissuing the book in hardcover. It was probably a vain hope. Bach had told him to forget it, but he still wanted to know how much it would take to get the plates.

Chapter 44

Eastman's reply came two weeks later. There were a number of surprises in the letter, but the biggest came in a short paragraph near the end:

"There are no plates to be transferred since this book was printed from standing type which, pursuant to normal trade practice, has been 'pied.' However, you could reproduce additional copies by photo-offset, once the rights have been reverted to your son."

Eastman's terminology meant that the book had been printed not from plates but on a press with movable type. A first—and last—printing of 4000 copies had been run on the press, after which the type had been "pied," or disassembled, as is normally done in the standing type process.

Hence, while the publisher would be restricted in its sale of a book to the number of copies in this first and only printing, the process was considerably cheaper than producing books from plates. But if the firm should subsequently want more copies of the same kind and quality to be sold at the same price, it would be forced to have the type set over again or have plates made. In either case the costs would be prohibitive, and thus the process was used only when a publisher had decided up front to market only a strictly limited number of copies. All of this would later be confirmed by people in the business, one of whom would also point out that, in order to at least recoup its investment in L.'s book, Prentice-Hall would probably have had to sell twice as many copies as were printed. L.'s own rough figures bore this out, and so it seemed clear that Eastman had decided on a printing program that promised his company a loss on the book right from the start.

This fact alone, however, was not necessarily incriminating. If asked for his reasons, Eastman would probably have claimed that he had wanted to avoid the larger loss which, in his professional judgment, the company would have incurred had the book been printed from plates and with a larger first run. He had simply decided its potential market was too limited. Besides, he might argue, his decision had not necessarily meant a loss on the book. The company might have made up its investment with the sale of subsidiary rights.

Still, L. would finally come to see Eastman's choice of a printing program as the one crucial decision that in a sense explained everything else the publisher had done to or for the book. The fact that only 4000 copies would be available for sale had automatically meant that the company's efforts in sales, advertising, and promotion — not to mention the book's own potential word-of-mouth — would be kept at something close to the minimum. And as a consequence, any hard-headed publisher would have been forced to consider the chances of selling subsidiary rights to book clubs, the movies, magazines, and paperback or foreign publishers to be practically nil. As a man knowledgeable in the business, Eastman could not have realistically entertained the notion that any such sales might net enough to recover Prentice-Hall's considerable investment in the book.

In a letter dated March 11, 1970 Tam Mossman had enclosed a dust jacket proof and had told L., "We are expecting galleys." So printing plans for the book must have been firmly established some weeks earlier, at some point in fact during those preceding five months when the book's progress had been delayed while Prentice-Hall's lawyers and then Eastman himself had supposedly pondered deletions and changes in the manuscript.

With his decision to run 4000 copies on standing type Eastman had chosen to scrap the book, and he had already done so when Mossman had told L. (near the end of March) that the company was pleased with the book and thought it should sell steadily over a number of years.

At that time, to L.'s knowledge, the only outside opinions on the book had been reported to the company by L. himself. It had been late in 1969 when he had given a copy of the manuscript to Mrs. Adler, Rabbi Groner, and a sociologist who was a member of Congregation Shaarey Zedek. Their response had been positive, and L. had passed them along to the publisher. But at that point word had no doubt traveled through certain circles in the community that a book on the assassination-suicide was soon to appear under the imprint of Prentice-Hall. And the essence of Mrs. D'Ark's story was that another member of the congregation had also undertaken to supply the company with an opinion, this one something less than positive.

Over the next several months, as L. considered Eastman's decision to print only 4000 copies of the book on standing type, more interesting ramifications seemed to emerge. For example, absurdity now hung on John Nelson's explanation of why the company had rejected a chance to sell 2000 copies to the Commentary Library. According to what he had told L., Nelson had informed the book club that at the price they were willing to pay, they would have to buy 10,000 copies of the book. But at that point, without plates and with a total inventory of something less than 2000 books, Prentice-Hall had no way of completing such a deal.

Most interesting of all, L. came to see that even on Eastman's own terms, his crucial decision had made no sense. Granting for the moment Eastman's contention that there had been no outside influence on the company and that his decision had been based simply on his perception of the book's market potential, just what were the circumstances surrounding that decision? The facts were that before officially giving the manuscript his final acceptance, and before he had okayed payment of the final $4000 of L.'s advance — both were first announced in the letter from Mossman dated March 11 — Eastman had already decided in effect to take a loss on the book. The question was then, why did Eastman decide to go ahead with publication when: 1) the contract was not yet legally binding, this being subject to the publisher's final acceptance of the manuscript; 2) the remainder of the advance owing to the author — upon final acceptance — had not yet been authorized; 3) the firm's attorneys were advising that a suit for invasion of privacy over the book was a distinct possibility; 4) the author had previously stated in writing that he was ready and willing to take his manuscript to another house if Prentice-Hall insisted on changes he could not accept; and 5) proceeding with publication with a total inventory of 4000 promised a money loss at least two times greater than would be incurred by terminating the contract and asking L. to go elsewhere?

To put it as simply as possible, Eastman had apparently possessed ample reason, under the circumstances, to find the manuscript unacceptable and refuse payment of the remainder of L.'s advance, to terminate the contract and in the process probably save his company several thousands of dollars. And yet he had not. Why? The only explanation L. now found reasonable was that the firm had responded to an outside suggestion to publish the book but keep it quiet, to offer it on the market but in a way that would keep its sale and public discussion at a minimum.

Fisher and friends in Detroit had evidently realized that if Prentice-Hall had refused to publish the manuscript, L. would simply have taken it to another house, one not as susceptible perhaps as Prentice-Hall to the influence they could muster. Thus, they had not tried to stop the book entirely but had instead prompted the company to minimize its public impact.

Chapter 45

Eastman's letter also contained a new plan for disposing of the book's remaining inventory. Prentice-Hall would first solicit bids from remainder houses (outfits that bought up publisher's overstocks or "remainders" and then sold them at greatly reduced prices). L. would then be given a chance to match the highest bid offered to purchase the approximately 1400 remainders if he so wished. If not, the company would sell them to the highest bidder after which the book could be declared out of print and all rights reverted to L.

As L. understood the procedure, remainders were commonly purchased for considerably less than the manufacturing cost of a book (in this case $2.25) with bids sometimes as low as a dime or a quarter per book. Thus, the upshot of the deal was that Prentice-Hall had dropped its demand that L. purchase the remaining inventory at $2.25 a piece and was offering him instead the option of buying the books for what would probably be much less.

The company's shift of position had been considerable—which was why, L. figured, its attorneys had probably insisted on the inclusion of Eastman's final paragraph:

> As to the next to the last paragraph of your April 10 letter, I must say in all honesty that I resent your attempt to pressure us into a settlement because of your allegation of the 'truth of the story' which you related to me in person in late March of this year. I told you face-to-face that there was no truth to the story; yet you have now taken the position that my denial was not true. Such an unwarranted assumption on your part is hardly the way to reach an amicable settlement of the entire matter. I have dealt with you in good faith, and I would like to

believe that you will act in the same manner.

L. was pleased that his demands had been met and felt Eastman was obviously saying the company had gone as far as it could go (without appearing too guilty). Still he was irked enough to write a long letter detailing the slips Eastman and D'Incecco had made in their recent encounter. He finally decided against sending it to Prentice-Hall and later would only be amused with the man's rhetoric: "I told you face-to-face..." There was apparently something about facial confrontation in this case that obviated the possibility of speaking false.

A few days later a letter from L.'s father agreed to the deal and made two further requests. Could Prentice-Hall send along a list of the names and addresses of those sent review copies and a list also of the places the company had approached about the possible sale of subsidiary rights? The information would be helpful in L.'s effort to promote the book on his own. Also, said L.'s father, since the company had agreed to repay half of the cost of the ad placed in the News and Free Press, he would much prefer to be reimbursed with the appropriate number of books.

Eastman replied subsequently that it would take a while to solicit and receive remainder bids, and within a few weeks — before a deal had been closed and the price of the book cut drastically--a total of 66 books would arrive in the mail; at L.'s forty percent author's discount they would be worth approximately $400, twice the amount owed.

Passover had arrived on April 10th, and, as she told L. the following week on the phone, JoAnn D'Ark along with her son, her husband, and her father had attended services at Congregation Shaarey Zedek.

"No matter what happens, my father always comes off smelling like a rose," said Mrs. D'Ark with a mixture of pique and admiration. Her father, she explained, had been accorded the high honor of reading from the Torah during the Passover service at the synagogue. Everyone had treated him with the usual cordial respect in the social hall after the service; and everyone had been courteous and friendly to Marv and their son as well.

"But no one, not a single person, said a word to me," said Mrs. D'Ark. "I walked up to people I've known practically all my life, and they just turned around and walked away. I almost called you up on Saturday to ask how a person goes about joining the Catholic

157

Church."

L. laughed but knew the experience must have been highly unpleasant for someone as comfortable in her community as Mrs. D'Ark. Her father, she said, had apparently come off as something of hero, because it was thought his role in keeping her story from reaching the public had saved the congregation from acute embarrassment.

And so L. now began to feel that their whole scene with Lou Gordon several weeks back had been arranged as a charade — a set-up to buy time for the offer of a "deal" and then to sidetrack and discourage them — with considerable help from Mrs. D'Ark's father. L. had given up on ever hearing from Gordon again and thought now that the Intrepid Reporter had either been handled or hoodwinked by close and trusted friends. Shortly Mrs. D'Ark would send Gordon a note that said that L. had an interesting story to tell about his confrontation with Prentice-Hall. Having never called Mrs. D'Ark to get her story, Gordon would maintain his silence, and L. would wonder again about the true extent of the commentator's role.

Since Julian Bach had finally refused to touch *Murder in the Synagogue*, by the end of April L. had approached two more literary agents in New York, sending each a copy of his book and a letter describing its background and asking the agent's services in selling its subsidiary rights as well as L.'s future work; also enclosed were a series of letters and documents which told the story of the book's suppression.

He had first tried a woman suggested by Bernard Rosenberg as "the hottest thing in New York," and then a man of solid reputation who had approached L. five years back after reading the Commentary piece and, unfortunately, after L. had already joined up with Jules Fields. "The list, as you may have heard, is very full," the woman had written in response; "it would be unfair of me--toward you--to suggest that I could work effectively in your behalf." The man had replied in a similar vein but added:

"I have seen many books poorly published--no ads, no review copies, little attention from the publisher--and it is not necessary to suppose that outside pressures were brought to bear in these cases. However, I cannot deny that something of a more purposeful nature may have happened to you and your book."

Chapter 46

In April L. exchanged letters again with Wertham and Coles and was grateful for their continuing encouragement and advice. Try sending copies of the book to selected magazines with a brief note telling its story and asking for a review, wrote Wertham. L. thought he would wait on that to see if he could swing a paperback deal. "You are beginning to write a piece right now--through your letters to me," enthused Coles. But in spite of L.'s casually tossed warning at the end of his lunch with Eastman and D'Incecco, he felt there were serious obstacles in the way of his story's publication.

"Right now I'm torn by the question of making this business public," L. had written to Coles. And for two months he debated whether there might be a way to publish the facts without causing more harm than good, in a fashion that hurt only the culprits.

The whole story turned on JoAnn D'Ark's report of Max Fisher's contribution to a conversation at a particular gathering. In order to effectively make her charges public, L. had originally felt she would have to attach her name to them, reveal the names of others at the gathering, and disclose where it had taken place. But as a matter of conscience, Mrs. D'Ark had ruled out giving any more information about the gathering, and attaching her name in public to her charges would immediately bring on the possibility of an ugly libel suit by one of the most powerful men in the country, a prospect she would have to face apparently without a single ally from that gathering. It also appeared that she would be ostracized by some of the people she had been closest to over the years, and the D'Arks, a quiet family who cherished their privacy, might be plunged into a maelstrom of unnerving publicity.

The question of Mrs. D'Ark's health had been resolved happily (tests had indicated not a recurrence of the illness she had fought off twice as a teenager, but a much less serious blood disease that would be treated without difficulty). Yet L. could hardly blame the D'Arks for remaining concerned about the consequences of making JoAnn's charges public: no one had the right to ask it of her.

Besides, he felt there was another factor, not much talked about between them, but perhaps an overriding consideration for Mrs. D'Ark—the role of her father. It now seemed quite clear that the man had been involved at least in the effort to protect Fisher. And further, L. had become all but convinced—from a few of her remarks and deductions of his own—that the gathering in question must have been a dinner party at her father's Southfield home. In effect then, JoAnn D'Ark feared the possibility that exposing the facts might mean publicly involving her own father.

The idea of Lou Gordon doing an investigative reporting job had been so appealing because she had thought, if Gordon's research satisfied him about her story, he might put his own reputation behind it and keep his source confidential.

This had proved a naive hope, and early in May L. finally called Mrs. D'Ark to explain that he had decided to forget any idea of trying to make the story public. There just seemed no good way to do it, and as soon as things were settled with Prentice-Hall, he would concentrate his efforts on getting the book into paperback.

The announcement made Mrs. D'Ark vehemently unhappy and later, unbeknownst to L., she called his father. Wasn't there something he could do? Why didn't he go ahead and sue Fisher and Prentice-Hall even though L., with no one to back her story, would probably lose? At least it would get the book a lot of publicity. They wouldn't necessarily lose on that point, said L.'s father. There were times when a jury believed one witness against the testimony of several others, but she would have to supply all the information she had. For one example, where this gathering had taken place.

"But that would involve my father," said JoAnn D'Ark almost to herself.

The matter was left unresolved, but the call prompted L. and his father to reconsider the chances of a suit. Over the next several months as L. continued to collect and correlate facts, legal action would come to seem increasingly feasible; the one sticking point, however, always remained the probable effect on the lives of Mrs. D'Ark and her family. Still, the vehemence of her reaction roused L. to think again about the possibilities of writing the story. Fiction he had quickly ruled out: it would not be enough to put a thin disguise on the story by changing the names of people and places and by altering some of the facts. That he was writing about the fate of his own book would show through all such camouflage. Only a substantial transformation of the material (to the point where it would really become a new story) would allow him to use it in a novel without being accused of trying to pump up *Murder in the Synagogue* with a scandalous story for which he apparently hoped to avoid responsibility. Some day he probably would use his experience with *Murder* in a full-fledged novel, but he was too close to it now and in no mood for that kind of project. No, it would have to be some kind of non-fiction approach.

On a nostalgic jaunt to Ann Arbor he sought out two of his former professors in the English department, told them his story and found them fascinated. Both urged him to write it down, in fact, this was the most obvious and logical thing to do. And L. too began to think he should at least get the facts down on paper, if only for "posterity," and even if they never reached publication. It would be good for the soul.

"It's the best story I know," he told his old American lit professor. "And I guess it's a good policy for a writer to always sit down and write the best story he knows."

Early in June he received a letter from the professor praising *Murder* and offering advice: "Do, if at all possible, carry through in one form or another with your account of subsequent events. I think a fair-minded reader would have to see that you've presented an impartial and un-malevolent account of the whole affair, and quite devoid of the sensational — the best sort of account of something well worth our attention."

L. had begun to write, but there would be a number of false starts and changes of direction over the next few months. He had intended to do an article but soon realized he had a book on his hands as he wrestled with the problem of how to tell the story persuasively without revealing Mrs. D'Ark's identity. Finally, he decided to write a closely detailed, thoroughly factual account, using pseudonyms only for the D'Ark family. This would not only protect the D'Arks in some measure but also offered L. more freedom in describing JoAnn's character and circumstances. Perhaps, if the reader could understand the woman and her position, and if L. could quote Rabbi Kapustin and maybe others on the subject of her integrity and reliability, the story might finally achieve its purpose.

As L. understood American libel law, in a case like this, involving the public interest, a man could have his say in public as long as he made a reasonable effort to check his facts and honestly believed in them. It wasn't as simple as that—there remained the small matter of finding a publisher—but L. had nonetheless set out to test the system. With a smile and a light touch of paranoia, he began telling friends: "If it comes to that, I can always make Xerox copies of the manuscript, and we can pass them around surreptitiously as the Russians do with their *samizdat*."

Chapter 47

At the end of May Eastman finally sent the two lists L. had requested a month earlier, one covering those outfits to which the company had offered the book for the possible sale of subsidiary rights, and the other naming those people to whom review copies had been sent.

The first list held no great interest for L., since John Nelson had already given him several minutes with a copy. In addition to the first serial magazines--Harper's, McCalls, True, and Commentary-- there were several newspaper supplements and syndicates indicated: few possibilities here for a difficult-to-excerpt book with no great topical interest. There were seven book clubs, twelve commercial paperback houses, and six film companies. Though Eastman's accompanying letter said, "We had no positive interest or offers from any of these," there, would be no way of ever really knowing what had gone on behind the scenes in these areas. The one outfit whose offer L. knew about, the Commentary Library, was not listed. Was that a secretary's oversight or had the Library made the first move?

The list of those sent review copies was another matter, and L. spent considerable time with it. At first glance, the eight pages of names and addresses were impressive, but the, longer and more care- fully L. looked, the more the initial impression faded. According to Pat Neger and later Eastman, the company normally sent out 300 promotion copies, but this list totaled only 173.

Of these, 16 were the author's request copies not sent until L. had said he would do so at his own expense. And 50 more had been sent to people scattered across the country (only two from Detroit) who had requested a copy in response to either a notice sent out by the company or some other mention of the book. Each of these requests had been considered individually by the publicity department, and books had been sent to about 15 small-time reviewers (from a rabbi at the Jewish Community Center in Saskatoon to a reverend at the

Soldiers and Sailors Home in Quincy, Illinois), a few radio and TV shows, and about 30 small-circulation newspapers and magazines (most of the reviews L. was aware of had come from these).

So that left a little over 100 books the company had supposedly sent out on its own initiative as review copies. Among these L. counted up a block of 35 sent to radio and TV shows on the East Coast. A half-dozen were network programs (the late-night talk shows were listed but not the Today Show — another secretarial oversight?). The rest seemed to include every local talk and interview show in Boston, New York City, Philadelphia, and Washington, D.C. But Pat Neger had said they would try the local shows only if they got a positive response from the networks. The one local show area she had mentioned was Pittsburgh. Well, thought L., these 35 names take up nearly two pages on this list, and in most cases there would have been promotion for the book only if the author had made an appearance, a possibility completely controlled by the publisher, since it, not the author, would receive requests.

With the radio-TV padding cut away, there were about 70 names left. Most were attached to city newspapers, tabloids, syndicates and news services. The rest, about 15 people, were either independent reviewers or connected with national circulation magazines or journals, from the Chicago Tribune's Book Week and the New York Times Book Review to, of course, the preview reviewers: Publisher's Weekly, the Library Journal, and the Kirkus Service.

In checking over the list, L. decided that if Prentice-Hall had done a thorough job for Max Fisher, about 20 of the recorded review copies had probably been "lost" on their way to the post office — specifically those intended for New York area reviewers and mass-circulation magazines and journals. To test his theory he sent letters to each of these, describing the book, indicating when it should have been received, and adding: "I've learned recently that unfortunate circumstances resulted in at least some of the review copies not being sent out." With each letter he enclosed a post card on which he had typed: "I received a review copy of *Murder in the Synagogue*... Yes___ No___ Not Sure___." The reviewer or editor had only to check the card appropriately, sign it and drop it in the mail.

He knew that many of these people might not keep records of the hundreds or thousands of books they received and that the passage of time (about nine months) might make a definite answer difficult or impossible. He also knew that some of them might be wary enough to simply toss his letter and card in a wastebasket. So L. was pleased when about half of those he had queried responded. Of the 20, one said yes: John Leonard's secretary at the New York Times Book Review said the book had been received on 8/24/70. So the TIMES really was the newspaper of record. Six marked unsure: those at Book Week, The New York Post, U.P.I., The Saturday Review Book Service, Publishers-Hall Syndicate and The Wall Street Journal. And two said no: John Chapman of the New York Daily News and Vincent Elefante of the New York Times.

One of those who had failed to respond to his letter was Christopher Lehmann-Haupt, a regular reviewer for the daily New York Times. This was the second unanswered letter L. had sent to Lehmann-Haupt. In May L.'s friend S. on a weekend visit to New York had found two copies of the book on a sale table of reviewers' copies in the basement of the Strand Book Shop. Inside the cover of one the books was the publisher's small envelope containing a reviewer's slip addressed to Lehmann-Haupt. S. had kept the envelope and given it to L., who found that still attached to the reviewer's slip was a mailing label which normally would have been fixed to the outside of the book's mailing box.

L.'s first letter to Lehmann-Haupt had been an effort to clear up the mystery of why the unused mailing label was still attached to the reviewer's slip. Had the reviewer received the book, and if so, how? By messenger service? Had he sold the unwanted review copy to the Strand, as was the custom with many reviewers in New York? Or had someone else taken the book and perhaps several other undelivered review copies and dumped them at the Strand and other New York book stores that dealt in such trade? Answers would never come.

Finally L. repeatedly combed the list Prentice-Hall had supplied looking for the names he felt obviously belonged but seemed to be missing, places where the book might have had its best chance of winning review space. It was clear in the end that, according to the company's own records, review copies had never been sent to most of the country's major popular and intellectual magazines and journals including: the New York Review of Books, Dissent, Partisan Review, The New Republic, The Nation, The National Review, The, New Leader, The New Yorker, The Atlantic, Harper's, Esquire,

Playboy, Psychology Today, Transaction, The Christian Science Monitor, and The National Observer.

Later in the summer L. would talk on the phone about this with Frank Tooni, who had left his job as director of trade publicity at Prentice-Hall in January. Tooni said it was normal practice for Prentice-Hall to send review copies to most of those magazines and journals.

L. told Tooni his story, and Tooni said he knew nothing about it. L. tended to believe him: Tooni had known next to nothing about the book when L. had first talked with him back in November, and it was no different now. Pat Neger had handled all the vital details.

Chapter 48

On June 17th L. wrote a letter to a man he was now fond of calling "Flash."

> Dear Mr. Gordon:
>
> I'm presently engaged in researching and writing the story of the events surrounding the publication of my book...and I wonder if you could provide some information.
>
> My question is this: Did Mr. Bob Yoder or anyone else representing Prentice-Hall, Inc., approach you or a member of your staff last fall about the possibility of my appearing on your TV show?...
>
> I intend my piece on this matter to be a patient and responsible documentation of the facts...it is scheduled for publication early next year.

The last line was of course designed to insure a response, and four days later L. received a call from Chuck Ferry, a member of Gordon's staff. A friendly voice on the phone, Ferry said they were anxious to have L. on the show as soon as possible because they felt the book was of considerable local interest and also because it was a matter of great interest to Lou himself. They were also very anxious to know more of what L. was writing about.

Ferry was either playing dumb or hadn't been told much by Gordon about L's previous contact with the show three months earlier, back in March. Ferry did say at one point that he had only been with Gordon since April. But in any case he was loaded with questions:

"Has this book been published?"

"Why haven't we heard anything about it?"

"Were there any reviews in the city?"

"Would you send us a copy of the review in the JEWISH NEWS and these other reviews from around the country?"

"It sounds like this book was suppressed. Is that what happened?"

"Do you know who did it?"

"Can you tell me who it is?"

"What are you writing about in the piece you referred to in your letter?"

"Do you have a publisher for it?"

L. answered the questions but withheld Fisher's name and fibbed about having a publisher.

About L.'s question Ferry said he had checked with Lou and the others on the staff, and no one recalled anyone from Prentice-Hall approaching them about an appearance. They would have booked L. right away, not only because of the local interest but also because of Lou's own acquaintance with Rabbi Adler. A while back Lou had made a few inquires about the book, said Ferry, but hadn't been able to learn much.

L. said yes, of course, he knew Lou had been contacted about the book's fate and had in fact talked with him about it. He had given Lou a copy of the book and a letter containing the publishing details but, not hearing again from him, had decided that Lou was very busy.

Ferry said nothing to this.

L. left open the question of appearing on the show, saying there would be no point to it now since there were no books in the stores. He was trying to arrange a paperback deal, and when that was settled he would get back in touch.

Fine, said Ferry, but two weeks later he called again. Lou had decided he wanted to do two shows with L. On the first, which they wanted to do as soon as possible, L. could talk about the suppression of the book. Then later when it became available in the stores, L. could come on again and talk about the book itself.

L. said he was sure Ferry could understand that, since he intended to write a careful and thorough account of the suppression, coming on the show now would only undermine his effort or at least diminish its effectiveness. Thus, he really wouldn't be interested in appearing until after he had finished writing the piece and probably not until after it was published.

"Frankly," he added, "it was never my idea to go to Lou with this story in the first place. The woman who called him about my book did so on her own, but I felt it was probably not the kind of story Lou could handle effectively. When we didn't hear from him, I decided that I had been right, that Lou's investigation had run into a dead-end, and that he had just dropped the subject."

Again Ferry made no comment, and L. was amused by this spectacle of the redoubtable Lou Gordon scrambling to rescue his badly tattered image as the Intrepid Reporter.

Chapter 49

At a dinner party with friends early in July, L. met a woman who operated a Little Professor bookstore in one of Detroit's northern suburbs. They talked about the book for a while, and at one point the woman said, "Well, I tried to reorder it a couple of times during the fall and the publisher sent me T.O.S. slips."

Temporarily out of stock. But according to L.'s reports from Prentice-Hall, the book had never been close to being out of stock, and the company warehouse still had 1400 copies. Perhaps, thought L., other stores in the area who had waited several weeks for orders to be filled during October and November had received similar messages.

Another bookstore operator whose shop was only a few miles from Congregation Shaarcy Zedek described the initial approach of Prentice-Hall's salesman in the area: "He said, 'You should probably take one of these, because, you know, it's about something that happened in the neighborhood.' And I said, 'Well, I've already sold one.' There was a rabbi a few doors down who used to come in all the time, and I knew he wanted the book. 'Don't you think maybe I should take three?' Of course, the first thing a salesman does is check the printing size, and if it's anything under 10,000, he knows he can forget about it."

In the second week of July L. received a letter from the Commentary Library rejecting the chance he had offered the club a month earlier to purchase up to 1300 copies of his book. A decision would have to be made soon on whether he would buy up the remainders from Prentice-Hall, and so he had written: "Since I'm primarily concerned with getting the book into the hands of people who might find it interesting and useful, I can assure you of an excellent price."

He had also reported John Nelson's account of Prentice-Hall's dealing with the club over the book and asked, "Is this your recollection of the matter?" And finally, he had included so many of the book's publishing details that any knowledgeable person would probably have guessed that something unsavory had been done to it. Perhaps this was why the letter from the club's general manager now seemed so circumspect:

"We have been considering the book and how we might use it and have concluded that it just does not work out right for the book club.

"That was our conclusion in our discussions with Prentice-Hall, but we reopened the matter after receiving your letter.

"I wish that I could be more helpful—but cannot at this time"

Below his signature the general manager had scribbled in red ink: "We are, of course, fully familiar with it through the article of yours that appeared in our magazine." An entirely needless postscript, thought L., which seemed to be saying, "If you think something unfortunate happened to your book, don't look at us. After all, we published your article on the same subject."

The termination papers, which cancelled L.'s contract with Prentice-Hall and returned the book's copyright to him, finally arrived in June. They stipulated, however, that the deal would not be final until September 1, when the company would officially declare the book out of print. This was necessary, Eastman had announced suddenly, in order to give the company's booksellers and outlets three months time in which to return for the full refund any books they might have purchased. Nonsense, thought L., Eastman's follow up proposal had clearly stated that upon a remainder sale the company would "immediately declare the book out of print and revert all rights to the author."

It was an issue he should probably fight them on, but he had little heart for more squabbling. With this stratagem the company had managed to drag out the settlement over five full months, and now it would be able to say that the rights had been reverted in this case nearly a year after publication--unusual but not extraordinary. Score one for Eastman and his lawyers.

Two bids had finally come in for the remainders, both a bit higher than L. had expected—72 cents and 96 cents. His father informed Eastman that they wanted to buy only 300 books and suggested that it might be a nice gesture for the company to send along at no cost another good-sized batch, because according to its own records it had sent out considerably fewer promotion copies than the 300 described as the norm.

On July 28th Eastman wrote back agreeing to the purchase, of 300 copies at 96 cents each. About the promotion copies he said many more than those listed had been distributed "via personal contact." As a matter of fact, he said, he had just checked the record and found that a total of 385 had been sent out. Even so, "in order to eliminate anything that would be considered a gray area," (L. laughed) he would send them fifty free copies.

L. had decided not to wait until September to offer the reprint rights for sale — by the time a decision would have to be made or a contract signed he would legally own the book. So in June with a measure of confidence he began sending out copies of his book along with cover letters and pages of excerpted quotes from personal letters and reviews. When no positive response had developed by the end of the summer, he tried again through the fall. In all he would approach fourteen commercial houses (publishers of the more popular pocket-sized softcover books) and about as many college-adoption and university presses. From the latter he received a prompt and consistent response: "Not suitable for our lists." Occasionally an editor might add: "A commercial press may well be interested..." But apparently the book had no appeal for the commercial houses either, since half of them never responded at all to L.'s approach, and the messages from those who did ranged from a printed slip saying: "At this time, Pocket Books is not able to consider unsolicited manuscripts for publication."

To this from Dell: "The non-fiction we do is usually on a subject which has already stirred nationwide interest (i.e., our books on Lt. Calley and the Pueblo commander). We do not feel that your book meets that requirement."

Also by the end of the summer he had tried three more agents in New York. With the first two, as with all of the reprint houses, he had said only that the book had been published in October 1970 and that he now owned it again. He wanted someone to help with the sale of subsidiary rights and also to handle his current work, a collection of short fiction and a non-fiction novel. The agents replied that they didn't handle "fragments of rights," as one of them put it. Neither mentioned his reference to "current work."

Finally, a writer friend sent a letter of introduction to a third agent, who had handled her work in the past, and L. sent along a brief description of the subject of his non-fiction novel-in-progress. This time there was no response at all.

Replete with the allure of paranoia, rejection is the writer's occupational hazard. But L.'s experience during the summer and fall more often involved a sense of incertitude and ambiguity as he pondered the cryptic notes or non-response of editors and agents and searched for a tip-off or a clue.

With the textbook and university presses he had no trouble viewing as genuine the argument that they were looking for books "of a more academic, scholarly nature for use in established college courses." But the response or lack of it from the agents and the commercial houses in New York had been more difficult to accept without some nagging suspicion. Especially after Julian Bach's words on the "publishing establishment" and the information L. continued to receive on the importance of the large distributors in the paperback industry.

One man, he had been told, controlled the sale of most mass market paperbacks in the state of Michigan. If word had gone out that this man had no intention of handling a book called *Murder in the Synagogue*, for example, its chances of reaching a commercial soft-cover edition were nil. Had this story become the subject of publishers' gossip in New York? (He had given the facts to four different agents.) Had reprint houses placed calls to the Michigan distributor or perhaps to Prentice-Hall? Was a rumor loose that someone in Detroit disliked this book, someone big enough to pressure one of the country's largest houses?

It was easy and tempting to assume that one of these things had happened to affect the book's chances. Yet L. could not be sure of it now, and the uncertainty, joined with his doubts over ever finding a publisher for his new tale, caused his writing to flounder occasionally.

There were moments too when he would wonder if he had not been naive and foolish in dealing with Eastman, if his book and perhaps everyone involved might not have been better served had he simply played the game, as Bach had strongly advised, accepting the facts of life about Corporate America and quietly exerting whatever pressure he could muster to get Prentice-Hall to run a little advertising, pump for some reviews, and sell the book to a reprint house and perhaps to the Commentary Library. This, or something close to it, was the deal Eastman had seemed to be offering.

Perhaps if he hadn't been so impatient and self-righteous, so anxious to prove his own moral superiority by wresting the book away from his sinful publisher...

But it was pointless to think that way. He had chosen his road, and he would travel as far as it would take him.

Chapter 50

At 8:40 on the morning of September 1st, L. answered his ringing phone and heard a warm and familiar voice saying, "Tom, this is Goldie Adler."

It had been eight months since he had spoken with the rabbi's widow, and during that time he had often debated whether or not to approach her with the subject of JoAnn D'Ark's tale.

Though he had finally decided he would have to, he knew he would put it off as long as possible. Mrs. Adler was the most widely revered and respected member of Congregation Shaarey Zedek and often thought of as the conscience of the community. To L. she had always seemed a remarkable combination of strong will, potent mind, and warm heart, a genuinely honest and authentic person. She had known nothing of the effort against the book, he was sure, and would have been outraged by it. He recalled his description of her in *Murder in the Synagogue*:

> A short buxom woman, her fine hair turning white and her dark eyes vivid and frank, Goldie Adler quickly communicates a gracious warmth and a practical, earthy wisdom. Her conversation is peppered with appropriate Jewish proverbs and humorous stories, but her intelligence is wide ranging and her moral indignation quick to surface. On Vietnam: "We send our boys over there and pin medals on them for doing the same things we'd throw them in jail for if they did them here." On a prominent national politician: "I've always thought he talks out of both sides of his mouth."
>
> On a popular "Jewish" novel: "I thought it was a rag, produced purely for profit, and I wrote the

author and told him so."

Those responsible, L. thought, must have kept the matter carefully from her, knowing with certainty she would not have stood for it, would no doubt have put a stop to it. But he recalled another, more troubling image from his book: the small determined woman moving quickly past 700 nearly hysterical people in the sanctuary of the synagogue to reach her husband of 36 years lying mortally wounded on the altar, shot in the head by a young man whom she and the rabbi had known well for several years. Mrs. Adler's secure and reasonable suburban life had been shattered in a few absurd seconds, and her memory of that horror had surely been unrelenting ever since.

This new story she could only find deeply upsetting; the people involved, including Max Fisher, were no doubt personal friends, and her position would be awkward and painful. These considerations had kept L. and Mrs. D'Ark from approaching Mrs. Adler in the first place. And yet now, though L. knew that she would be hurt, it would simply be unfair if he made this story public without first giving her the details and without asking if she could vouch for Mrs. D'Ark's integrity and support her action.

Early in the summer Mrs. Adler and L.'s mother had met briefly at one of the performances of the Metropolitan Opera in Detroit. The rabbi's widow had asked how the book was doing, and his mother, her maternal instincts inflamed, had said not very well because there had been an effort to suppress it. There had been no time for details or explanations, and now on the phone L. was sure that his mother's remark at the opera was one of the things on Mrs. Adler's mind.

She had been meaning to call for some time, she said, but she had been out of town for much of the summer and had also spent time in the hospital having an ulcer removed. She wondered if he had seen the fine review of the book in the Reconstructionist—the journal of the liberal wing of Conservative Judaism.

It had recently reprinted Rabbi Riemer's review, and L. said, yes, he'd been very pleased. He went on to joke that she had called on an important day in the book's history: the date it was to be officially declared out of print. From there they launched into a discussion that finally extended over two lengthy phone conversations and covered nearly every facet of the book's fate.

As it turned out, Mrs. Adler had thought his mother had been referring to the fact that some people in the community who had not read the book had talked against it and on occasion had done things like have it removed from the shelves at the Jewish Book Fair. She had heard that these people had said they were acting out of a concern for the Wishnetskys and for her, but she had always made it very clear that she fully approved of the book:

"When someone would come to me and say, 'I don't know why they ever published such a book,' I would say, 'You should read it. Read the epilogue first, and you'll know why it was written. And then read the whole book.'"

L. said he had been told of her strong support and had never doubted it. But the effort of a handful of people against the book had extended much further than she was describing, had actually reached all the way to the publisher. He proceeded to fill in the details of the story, and after the obvious initial shock and dismay, after he had read from his informant's letter to Fredric Wertham, and after the rabbi's widow had recalled that in years past she herself had taught the young woman in a Sunday school class, there was no hesitation or qualification about Mrs. Adler's endorsement and support of JoAnn D'Ark as an honest and responsible person.

Of course, this woman had told L. the truth, she said; it was impossible to believe that she would ever make up such a story. L. said he felt Mrs. D'Ark's letter to Wertham was a beautiful and rare act of moral courage. Mrs. Adler fervently agreed.

They talked at length about the hows and whys of the book's suppression, and though she said she had always thought of book publishing as "sacrosanct," Goldie Adler quickly understood how even in this area of American business, manipulation could be achieved with certain kinds of power and influence. She also seemed to agree with L.'s analysis of the motivation of those responsible. As for Max Fisher, there had been a two or three second pause after L. had used the name for the first time, after which she had said, "Well, he's the last person I would have thought of." She knew him very well—she had been sitting in his seats, in fact, the night she had met L.'s mother at the opera—and he was a good man, she thought. She couldn't imagine how he had brought himself to do such a thing. "Of course," she chuckled with irrepressible wit, "I've never crossed him."

The revelations had obviously hurt and angered Mrs. Adler, but typically she was still thinking of others. L. shouldn't feel too badly, she said; after all to receive such attention was a kind of flattery. And she recalled how in 1935 Rabbi Adler had received a letter, apparently sent to every Jewish pulpit in the country at the time, urging that a new book entitled *Call It Sleep*, by a young writer named Henry Roth, be completely ignored. L. had read and loved the book, a brilliant first novel of Jewish immigrant life, when it had been rediscovered and reissued in soft-cover back in the early '60s. And he knew the sad story behind the book, how the young author's ego had been shattered when both publisher and public had ignored his effort and he had managed to write almost nothing ever since.

Later, when L. mentioned that Mrs. D'Ark had been feeling somewhat isolated, Goldie Adler immediately asked for the young woman's phone number.

Shortly thereafter, a pleased JoAnn D'Ark called L. to report a long, reassuring chat with Mrs. Adler. "I told her, 'I don't feel like I deserve compliments. I've had many weak moments. Sometimes I've wondered if what somebody told me once wasn't true — that I should have deferred to the wisdom and better judgment of my elders.'

"And Mrs. Adler said, 'But do you think it was right for people to do something like this?'

"And I said, 'No, I don't.'

"And she said, 'Then, of course, you did the right thing. Just remember that it's not always easy to do the right thing when you have to go against the tide.' And she talked about how Rabbi Adler would have been shocked and outraged at something like this."

Chapter 51

From the library at Illinois Tech, L. called Bob Yoder at his apartment in a high-rise building on the other end of the campus. Yoder suggested lunch at the student center cafeteria and gave directions. "You'll recognize me," he said. "I have only one arm."

Under a bleak gray sky, L. walked across the campus, almost deserted because of the year-end holidays, a large treeless place with many uninspired new buildings on what seemed to be urban renewal land in one of Chicago's predominantly Black neighborhoods. At the cafeteria Bob Yoder materialized as a man of about 60 with thick gray hair and a full mustache. He seemed naturally affable, though a bit leery perhaps about just what L. was up to. After cheeseburgers for which Yoder insisted on paying, he smoked several cigarettes, lighting matches adroitly by holding the match book down with whatever he had in his coat sleeve.

At the end of the summer L. had spoken with Yoder twice on the phone from Detroit and had received some interesting information along with the feeling that a personal visit might bring something more. He had chosen not to tell Yoder that he was writing the history of his book, only that he was investigating rumors about its being suppressed. Nick D'Incecco had said back in March, "Bob Yoder is no longer working for us full-time." But L. did not know the man's current status with the company and had decided to be cautious. As he learned later, Yoder no longer had any connection with Prentice-Hall and was selling and promoting for a number of other large houses. On the phone in August Yoder had outlined his experience with *Murder in the Synagogue*, and now in person he filled in details.

As instructed he had come to Detroit in the fall of 1970 and had made the rounds to the appropriate radio and TV shows in the area in an effort to arrange appearances for L. He had been successful in getting a specific date on the Morning Show and a tentative arrangement with J.P. McCarthy's Focus Show on WJR radio. Yoder

179

had called this information in to Pat Neger and had also sent her written reports for each show.

To his surprise, however, he had not been successful with the Lou Gordon Show. He had thought the book ("a local story by a local author") was a natural for the Gordon show and couldn't understand the resistance he was getting from Gordon's staff. In addition, said Yoder, he had read the book and thought it a very solid piece of work and had given it his personal recommendation to the young woman who was Gordon's assistant producer. But while his recommendation in the past had been enough to sell the Gordon staff, he could not secure a commitment for this book.

Soon after the first of the year Yoder made another visit to Detroit, and though he made another tentative arrangement, this time with Woman's World (a TV show produced in Windsor, syndicated by the CBC all over Canada, and seen in a number of U.S. border cities), he again got nowhere with the Gordon staff. He left a copy of the book with them, but the manner in which his approach had been turned away had fostered the "definite feeling" that the show had been "pressured" into not booking L.

Subsequently, late in January, Yoder was assigned to escort another Prentice-Hall author, Selma Diamond, whose book *Nose Jobs for Peace* had also been published in the previous fall, to a sisterhood luncheon-lecture at Congregation Shaarey Zedek. During the luncheon, said Yoder, he talked about L.'s book with a number of women in the congregation. Their attitude was that, especially out of a concern for Mrs. Adler, "to spare her," the book should not be given attention so soon after the shooting. "Maybe in the next generation," they said.

Yoder had also spoken at some length with Mrs. Adler, who brought him on a tour of the synagogue, showing him the sanctuary and pointing out the place on the bimah where the rabbi had been shot. L. was a delightful young man, Mrs. Adler had said, and his book was well researched and well-written. Unfortunately, she said, there were members of the congregation whose feelings were still raw and who were upset by the book's appearance. It had just come too soon for them. Yoder left the synagogue feeling confirmed in his hunch that some kind of pressure had been put on the Gordon show by someone connected with the congregation.

In reporting to Pat Neger soon afterward, he had mentioned his suspicions about the book's fate in Detroit, particularly with the Gordon show. Miss Neger had told him to "forget it," said Yoder, and he had replied, "Well, that's no way to sell books. Something could still be done for this book. You don't just give up and walk away because a book seems to be a little controversial and has some people against it. There's no reason to be afraid of a little controversy." According to Yoder, Miss Neger had again told him to simply drop the matter.

L. left Chicago feeling that Yoder had given him straight answers, even though it might have been safer for the promotion man to say nothing that might reinforce the idea of the book's suppression.

By now L.'s kindest interpretation of Gordon's role in the story was that the man had been duped, probably by close friends, first during the fall about the desirability of having L. on the show, and then several months later about the credibility of Mrs. D'Ark's story. Some months earlier, on Lou's fifth anniversary show, a number of his closest friends had made special appearances. One of them had been Max Fisher.

Chapter 52

L. walked several blocks through a late-morning mixture of rain and snow past Carnegie Hall to the Seventh Avenue entrance of the Hotel Wellington. Inside the heavy glass doors he stopped and applied his handkerchief to his fogged and spattered gold-rimmed spectacles. Like many of his American contemporaries with new glasses, new clothes and new hair styles, he had altered his appearance somewhat over the past five years. He wondered how quickly recognition would come with the man who was supposed to be waiting for him in the Wellington lobby.

On the phone the night before, Jules Fields' voice had sounded friendly but weak, the agent quickly explaining that he had been quite ill for the past three weeks and remained in very poor health. L. had commiserated and said he hoped that Fields would be feeling better soon. The man had sounded as if he hardly expected to recover.

"It's a hell of a thing," Fields had said, "to be sick and to be all alone over Christmas and New Years. You know, I'm all alone, and there's no one to take care of me except me." His voice was miserable and pleading for pity, and L. was somewhat relieved to hear finally that, though Jules was suffering with a lingering bout of the Hong Kong flu, he would be happy to meet and chat with L. the following day.

In the lobby recognition was prompt and mutual. L. found Fields sitting near the newsstand, talking with a woman who worked at the hotel. Gray and unshaven, the agent looked sickly as he struggled to his feet and barely managed a smile. After L. phoned his former editor Gladys Carr about seeing her later in the day, he and Fields moved to a couch and a chair on the other side of the room, and they got down to business.

L. explained that he had come to talk to Fields and Miss Carr about the new book he was writing on the suppression of *Murder in the Synagogue.* Fields revealed no surprise or curiosity. L. recalled that his wife's cousin Margaret, who had been his original contact with Fields, had been in New York about six weeks earlier and had given the agent some of L.'s story. Margaret had reported to L. that Fields had gone immediately to Miss Carr (or so he had said) and had learned that as of the time she had left Prentice-Hall, the company was high on the book and planning a good solid promotion campaign.

Now, however, Fields said nothing of having talked about the book with Miss Carr and instead offered a tale of how he had fought with Prentice-Hall and had not been in touch with the company for some time. He had been on particularly bad terms with Wilbur Eastman, he said. In fact he had gone to Prentice-Hall in March, 1970, and had argued with Eastman specifically about L.'s book. Eastman had told him that he was ordering a first run of 5000 copies, and Jules had ended up telling the trade division president that he didn't know anything about the book business. He had not been back to Prentice-Hall and had not spoken with Eastman since.

"If that happened in March," said L., "then at about the same time or soon after they were slandering you to me. I was told about the end of March by Tam Mossman that I should sever my connection with you because you were more or less out of the business and because they had been having some difficulty getting checks through you to their authors."

Jules Fields had no comment and changed the subject. Later, however, L. returned to the matter of that March meeting: "I would have appreciated hearing from you about what you learned from Eastman. At least, you know, it would have warned me and given me some indication of what was going to happen."

Once again Fields acted as if he hadn't heard L.'s comments. He began coughing and complained again about how miserable he felt. Later L. tried once more to focus on what concerned him most about the agent's role in the story.

"So when you went to Eastman in March and learned what their plans were, you just decided the book wasn't going anywhere, and that's why..."

This time Fields didn't let him finish. "Tom," he interrupted, "send me both books, and I'll see what I can do for you." He would not be able to get L. very much for the paperback rights to *Murder in*

183

the Synagogue, he said, as if the intervening five years since they had last seen each other had never happened. About the chances of the new book he would have to withhold his opinion until he had taken a look at it.

L. explained that he had already approached most of the paperback houses without success and outlined briefly the case made by his new book.

What happened at Prentice-Hall, said Fields, acting again as if he hadn't heard L.'s remarks, was that since the book had started out as Gladys Carr's project, it had been written off and forgotten when she left the company.

They fenced briefly, and L. was both amused and annoyed with the old man's transparent attempt to discourage him about the new book and his slippery refusal to answer or even listen to questions. Fields said he was feeling terrible and should never have gotten out of bed today. He was sorry to have to cut their meeting short, but he just didn't have much strength left and would have to go up to his room and lie down.

"Send me the new book, and I'll tell you what I think," he repeated.

L. said he'd have to think about that, and Fields, shifting his position quickly, gave him the name of an editor at Doubleday to whom he should send the manuscript. L. wrote down the name as one to avoid.

Jack, another old Wellington regular, stopped by to ask how Jules was feeling this morning. "This is one sick boy," he told L., and Fields rose unsteadily to his feet, took his leave, and shuffled slowly off to the elevator with his friend.

Later over a cup of coffee at the counter in the hotel drugstore, L. berated himself for being soft and sentimental with Fields. The old man had made a fool of him, playing for his pity, giving him little chance to ask his tough questions, and not even acknowledging the ones he had managed to ask. And for some reason he had been polite to the crafty old dodger from beginning to end. Why hadn't he been able to get off a few simple direct questions?

"Why did you drop me and pass up your $400 share of the remainder of my advance?"

"Exactly what did Eastman tell you about the book in March, 1970?"

"Did he scare you off by telling you that this book was trouble or did he pay you a little something to get lost?"

L. told himself that Fields would never have answered anyway. The interesting thing was this story about a meeting between Fields and Eastman in March. It meant that Mossman — no doubt on orders — had told L. that Fields was "more or less out of the business" just shortly after the agent had supposedly been fighting with the company over L.'s book.

Even more interesting was the fact that the company must have been certain of its position vis-a-vis Jules Fields when it suggested to L. that he keep the $400 legally owed to the agent and then slandered the man. In other words, Eastman must have already fixed matters with Fields before L. was advised to sever their connection. Otherwise, if L. had gone to the agent with Prentice-Hall's story about him, trouble might have brewed.

Later, after browsing a bookstore, where he bought his friend DeBusschere's book newly issued in paperback, and lunching at a delicatessen, L. rode a cab to McGraw-Hill to speak with Gladys Carr.

It would be some weeks yet before the company's massive building on 42nd Street would be awash with the scandal of Clifford Irving's plot to dupe the world with his Howard Hughes hoax. The story would do little for the credibility of other writers with even slightly unusual tales to tell. To what lengths would L. have to go, he would wonder, to prove his story true: trial by fire, Chinese water torture, an interview under Sodium Pentothal on the Lou Gordon Show? L. had little use for pain, but the truth serum might be fun if Lou would agree to share it with him and invited Max Fisher and Wilbur Eastman to come on and do the same. More seriously, since Lou was a strong believer in the efficacy of polygraph tests, perhaps L. would arrange a test for Mrs. D'Ark and himself (she was more than willing) from an operator who couldn't be bought or pressured.

Gladys Carr had moved up in the world, from the basement at Prentice-Hall to the twentieth floor at McGraw-Hill as editor-in-chief of its American Heritage Press. If the woman had not come up to him in the reception room wreathed in smiles and calling his name, L. would not have recognized her. They had met only that one time at the Plaza five and half years earlier, and in the interim she appeared to have gained perhaps fifteen pounds, and her dark blond hair had acquired a strawberry hue. She looked good, L. thought, in a beige pantsuit and with a ruddy, healthy complexion and sedately modish octagonal glasses. On her left hand, he noticed what looked to be a wedding ring.

In her large office with a fine view of Manhattan, it took only a few friendly minutes to establish that she knew nothing of L.'s book—not even that it had been published. No, she had not talked about it with Jules Fields, and in fact, she and Fields had lost touch with one another until a couple of weeks back when they had bumped into each other by chance in a drugstore. So much for Fields' story of having gone to Miss Carr to learn what he could about the book for cousin Margaret.

The book had not yet gone to production when she had left Prentice-Hall, she said, and at that point she had no real indication of Eastman's attitude or plans. It was Eastman, she confirmed, who made all important decisions on trade division books at Prentice-Hall.

After L. had related a few of the details, Miss Carr seemed to have no trouble accepting his story. She thought he was wrong, however, in thinking that someone over Eastman in the company hierarchy had received the initial approach from Max Fisher and had authorized the squelching. Ticking off the names at the top of the firm, she eliminated each as one who might have done Fisher a favor. Eastman, however, was a different story, she thought, especially since he had been acquainted with Fisher and had dealt with him before.

Something like this, said Gladys Carr, happened occasionally in the publishing industry, and no one in the establishment was going to be very interested in offering the public a book about it. Those small houses outside the establishment would probably lack the where-with-all to face up to the possible legal challenge. Give it a chance at publication, she said, and write it as fiction.

Chapter 53

There had been other times, social occasions, most notably opening night of the Metropolitan Opera in Detroit in the previous May, when a personal encounter between L. and Max Fisher had seemed a possibility. But none had appeared as promising as the preview opening of a new college theater venture that L. and his wife attended early in February. Max and his wife were listed with the honorary chairmen in the program an inch away from L.'s parents who were serving as working co-chairmen. An appearance by the Fishers at the preview seemed likely.

In the past year L. had indulged in occasional reveries of what a chance meeting with Fisher might be like, fantasizing moments in which he would give the man the silent treatment perhaps—a cold, venomous stare or the enigmatic smile? Or would he offer a whimsical remark? Something like, "Oh, yes, Mr. Fisher, I've heard so much about your extraordinary interest in my book."

Of course, there had always been the possibility of just picking up the phone and calling Max Fisher or arranging a meeting or just writing a letter. Certainly the book he was close to finishing could use for its climactic scene a confrontation between the Financier Prince and the Young Author Wronged. According to L.'s wife, it might even serve some therapeutic purpose to cut the man badly with a few quick verbal thrusts.

The trouble was that L. felt he had really nothing to say to Fisher, at least nothing that promised to affect the man in some significant way. When he tried to imagine a serious speech, he came off sounding pompous and self-righteous, saying things that Fisher would probably find incomprehensible anyway. No, he would not arrange a meeting simply for a theatrical or self-indulgent purpose, especially since it probably made more sense to keep the man guessing from rumors about the information L. now possessed and what he planned to do with it.

At the theater preview the Max Fishers failed to appear. L. and his family, however, did sit across the aisle from Frank Angelo, whose office in the editorial department at the Free Press L. had visited ten days earlier. With a notion that it might be easier to find a publisher for his new book if the paper would do a solid investigative reporting job and then run the story, L. had decided to test reactions at the Free Press.

The Republican News, with its close ties to Fisher, was a hopeless case. Even so, L.'s mother had mentioned the suppression in chatting recently with Nancy Manser, the religion editor at the News. Miss Manser had seemed interested and had asked for a copy of the book. L.'s mother had personally delivered one to the News, but Miss Manser had never acknowledged its receipt.

At the Free Press L. had outlined his story for his father's old friend Angelo and had met with considerable skepticism. He had personally known the leaders at Congregation Shaarey Zedek, including Max Fisher, for many years, said the short, stocky, white-haired Angelo, and he found it almost impossible to believe that any of them would get involved in such a thing. Of course, every young author thinks his book is the most important thing that's ever been published and feels everyone should be deeply interested in it. The facts, however, are a little different.

L. pointed out that he was not exactly bringing the Free Press a raw rumor that he wanted printed as the gospel. He had spent nearly a year investigating and writing the story and felt he had proceeded with care and caution. Now he was only asking if the Free Press would be interested in looking over the facts he had gathered and perhaps doing an investigation of its own.

Look, said L., neither he nor his book was important in this story. What was significant was that the action taken against this book seemed typical of something that was happening all too often in American society, the kind of covert manipulation, practiced by men and organizations of inordinate power and influence, that frequently tampered with individual hopes, plans, and efforts. The story might sound shocking because the suppression of a book wasn't supposed to happen in America, and one usually heard only about those attempts that failed and attracted a lot of attention.

But this kind of thing went on everyday in the business world when a concern for image, or for anything that might mean a loss of dollars, moved one man to pressure another or simply to ask for a break or a favor in exchange for future considerations. And that's all this was, a business deal, because Prentice-Hall was one of those large corporations in the publishing industry, many of them now part of giant conglomerates, obviously subject to various kinds of business pressures. It seemed clear, said L, that if a man could simply pick up a telephone and accomplish such a thing—and that was probably how it was done, with just a phone call—then it was a matter to be concerned about. And if one should come up with enough evidence to tell such a story persuasively, then it should be told and as widely as possible.

Angelo agreed and said, of course, if L.'s assertions could be reasonably documented, the Free Press would be most interested in the story. L. left the editor a selection of excerpted quotes on the book and a typed, three-page, single-spaced summary of the "salient facts." Angelo said he would read through the material and get back to L. and would also like a chance to read the book.

At the theater a week and a half later the editor told L.'s father that he was reading the book and would want to talk to L. again when he had finished. Before proceeding, Angelo would probably have to discuss the matter with others at the top echelon of the Free Press. After another twelve days had passed, L. encountered Angelo again, this time at a benefit showing of the new DeSica film, "The Garden of the Finzi-Continis," another of his parents' projects, this one raising a fund to save Venice from crumbling into the sea. They met briefly at the door on the way out, and the editor gave him a quick nervous smile. L. knew he would not hear from the Free Press again.

After the film, a quietly moving story of the Italian Jews of Ferrara at the outbreak of World War II, L. found himself caught up in questions about his own relations with the Jewish community. If his new book ever reached the public, was it likely to be misused by the sick and the vicious? And despite his stated purpose, might he be marked with the shameful name of anti-Semite?

Certainly the fact that books were sometimes misused was a matter over which their authors usually had little control. He could only try to make his points as clearly and as carefully as possible, emphasizing that blame should be attributed only to a few at Shaarey Zedek, a tiny minority not only of Detroit's Jewish community but of the congregation as well.

From one of the wealthiest men in the congregation to an ultra-Orthodox Hasid, a wide range of people in the community had given him warm support and generous help during his research and writing. With its hundreds of Jewish contributors, the book itself stood as solid evidence of the community's openness and good will, its lack self-isolation and paranoia. And after publication, praise for *Murder in the Synagogue* had reached L. in a thin but consistent pattern from nearly every segment of the Jewish community, from rabbis, psychiatrists, academics, doctors, lawyers, judges, businessmen and housewives, from young people and old alike.

No, those few who had acted against the book were not typical. Their attitudes were shared only by a handful of people who were sadly out-of-touch, wrapped perhaps in fears from the past and misperceptions of the present. Their real concern seemed less for the Jewish community than for their own peace of mind.

Max Fisher's own attitude might have been somewhat different. A man of extraordinary influence and power, he had apparently been asked to perform what was simply considered a needed exercise in cosmetics. Perhaps without giving it much thought, he had done so, in the process no doubt pleasing and impressing his old friends in the congregation.

L. wondered if, upon greater reflection, the man would come to understand that in reaching out to a stranger over a wall she had lived behind most of her life, JoAnn D'Ark had proved that the ancient moral genius of her people could still live vitally in the suburbs of Detroit.

Chapter 54

There would be those who would say that morality was a relative matter, that Max Fisher's philanthropy, tax-deductible though it was, had performed far more good for people than anything either L. or Mrs. D'Ark could ever hope to accomplish. It was, they would argue, cruel and unfair (not to mention self-serving) to scandalize the great man's name for little more than a thoughtless mistake. But putting aside the private motives of public philanthropy or the qualities of character that might prompt one to squelch a book, L. felt there was at issue here something real and important.

It was often observed now that the American people were enveloped in a crisis of confidence, a sense that their major institutions had become inadequate and unresponsive to their will and needs. One common concern was that those institutions were increasingly controlled by small numbers of powerful, arbitrary and deceitful men who did not hesitate to impose their personal values or to protect their own positions of wealth and influence by using the favor, the pay-off, the cover-up and the lie, by pulling strings behind-the-scenes, by covering much of the nation's public life with a massive web of fraud and deception in the interest of the status quo.

And so a profound distrust of authority and leadership at all levels of American society had grown more rapidly than anyone might have predicted over that troubled decade of the 1960s.

Yes, at the heart of the matter were the perennial concerns of truth, illusion and the corruption of power. But in a mass society founded on democratic principles, these matters often seemed much more complicated and confusing than in the past. The breakdown of trust and confidence in leaders and institutions had fostered a dangerous sense of individual impotence in the face of America's social, political and ecological problems.

The poison of doubt and dissolution was in the air, pumped there by the failures of both men and institutions, infecting relations between citizen and government and between groups in society, and seeping even into that private relationship between a man and himself. For the false, the misleading and the manipulative made ever more difficult and confusing the individual's effort to render valid judgments not only on the realities of society but also on the true shape of personal identity.

L. thought that those who had acted against his book, or who had rendered their assistance or complicity, had sent another small dark cloud of deceit into an atmosphere already badly tainted. The menacing fact in his tale was that, though these people might not have been prompted by base or evil motives, they apparently remained unaware that the American social and political environment might be cleared and freshened only if those in positions of public trust somehow developed and demonstrated JoAnn D'Ark's courage to speak and act on the truth.

There seemed little chance of that happening, L. thought. But in this case, as that familiar mantra of the young observed, if you weren't working on the solution, you were part of the problem.

EPILOGUE

If I had not seen the photograph in a Detroit newspaper a while back, you would probably not be reading this. It showed an older gentleman with a thick build, lots of white hair and a rather distinguished looking mustache and goatee. There was something vaguely familiar about him.

The caption said he was Leo McNamara, performing in a new play at the Purple Rose Theater in Chelsea, Michigan, just outside Ann Arbor. The Purple Rose had been founded several years earlier by the Hollywood movie actor Jeff Daniels.

As I gazed at the photo I wondered if this might be the same Leo McNamara who was my first literature professor at the University of Michigan after I arrived in Ann Arbor, having transferred from Notre Dame in the middle of my junior year. Almost 40 years had passed since those days, and the Leo McNamara I recalled was a lean, clean-shaven young man with short dark hair. He had come from Harvard the year before my arrival on campus. Intense, erudite and insightful, he nonetheless remained in my memory as a somewhat shy, less-than-comfortable presence in front of my class in American lit. Could that Leo McNamara have become the Leo McNamara in this photo, comfortable enough in front of an audience to perform as a professional on stage?

I was tough on my lit professors in those days. One, a respected lecturer in the Russian novel, had so disappointed me with what I felt were pedestrian observations on some of the world's most exciting and important works of literature that I simply stopped going to his class. I read the books, wrote and submitted my papers and bluebook exams and got my grade, an A as I recall.

But I liked Mr. McNamara. His mind was quick, agile, wide-ranging and unconventional. At Harvard, in addition to his lit studies, he had been involved in research psychology. At Michigan he would soon be lecturing as well in Irish history. To my iconoclast's delight, he had no Ph.D. and no intention of getting one.

So after I finished his American lit class, we stayed in touch. We'd meet occasionally both on and off campus through my graduate year at U. of M. and for several years after I left Ann Arbor. I'd show him my writing, first short stories and later non-fiction, including *Murder in the Synagogue*, and I always valued his opinion. Finally in the early '70s, I gave him my last copy of *JoAnn D'Ark and the Prince Of Detroit*. I appreciated the encouraging things he said about the manuscript, but for some reason thereafter I stopped calling Leo McNamara, and our connection was broken.

So why did I give away my last copy? As you've probably surmised, I had separated myself from the book to help put an obsessive, all-consuming experience totally behind me. In short, I needed to move on with my work and my life. In the years that followed I also divorced and changed careers. But those were moves I shared with many other Americans of my generation, and that's another story.

So what moved me, after all that time, to see if the two Leos were one and the same, and perhaps then to learn if, by some miraculous chance, he had managed to hold on to that lost manuscript while passing through more than three decades of our throw-away society?

I guess the simple answer is age. Pushing into my 60s, I had finally begun to peek back very occasionally at a life that had been both highly compartmentalized and relentlessly devoted to moving forward. Old friends, schoolmates, lovers, acquaintances and co-workers, as well as favorite restaurants, homes, workplaces, institutions, habits and beliefs, once finished with and left behind, were, for the most part, simply not revisited, re-acquired, or reviewed.

But now moved by those common intimations of mortality that inevitably come with one's 60s, I finally took a few minutes to write an email with the subject line: "Looking for Leo." I sent it to a woman at U. of M. who helped administer the university's Hopwood student writing awards. I had won one of those awards 40 years ago, and I knew that Leo had often served as a judge.

Though I had never shared any information with the Hopwood folks over the years, they had kept track of me for four decades, sending out their annual newsletter packed with personal and professional info about current and former winners. Now my e-mail mentioned the photo I had seen of a Leo who looked like he could be my old professor-friend Leo. Might the Hopwood office have contact info?

The reply came quickly. Oh, yes, Leo had often mentioned me over the years. Included were a phone number and an email address. And so the relationship resumed. After 30 years there was a good deal of catching up to do, and nearly every week at the old Cottage Inn restaurant in Ann Arbor we've been catching up ever since.

Of course, sooner rather than later the subject of the lost book came up. "Oh, of course I have it, Tommy," said Leo, his dark eyes dancing. "As I told you back then, it's a very good book."

The new, older Leo was pushing 70, his mind still sharp and vigorous, his white hair curling over his collar, and now he seemed totally at ease with himself. With two wives and nine children, he had lived an extraordinarily full life...up, down, inside out and occasionally backwards. A marvelous raconteur and story-teller, Leo loved talking about all of it. Retired from the university, he still lectured on Irish history during the summer and taught literature to students at a local law school. Acting with a number of theater companies in the area had been great fun for years, but he wasn't doing much of that any more. Instead, he was day-trading on his computer at home. He wasn't greedy, he explained. He was fine with a thousand bucks a week.

Knowing from sad experience that there's a difference between thinking you possess something and actually being able to put your hands on it, I hesitated to push my new old friend to bring the old manuscript to one of our lunches. But after several weeks, when our chat turned briefly to the book again, I asked if he really thought he could find it. Of course, said Leo, he'd bring it along next week.

And sure enough at our next lunch he was carting a thin white plastic grocery bag filled with a battered but totally familiar orange Eaton typing paper box. It and its contents had survived intact moves between his office at the university and two different residences. Over the years he had mentioned the book to a half-dozen different friends who expressed a desire to read it. Each time he gave it away, and each time it came back. Now it was finally back in my hands.

It would be quite a while before I actually opened the box and proceeded with the task of scanning the full manuscript into my computer. Of course at that point I read my book for the first time in over 30 years, cringing more than a few times with embarrassment at my own foibles and foolishness. Eventually, I would give the book one more careful edit, clarifying some murky prose, condensing a few overblown portions of the text, but changing nothing substantial. My intent remained the same as when I first wrote the story: borrowing that hackneyed line from countless TV courtroom dramas, to tell the truth, the whole truth, and nothing but the truth.

"Max M. Fisher, the son of Russian immigrants who scaled the heights of power in business, politics, and philanthropy, died Thursday at his home in Franklin at the age of 96."

As the headline story noted in the Detroit News coverage of his passing, at about 11:30 in the morning on March 3rd, 2005, Max Fisher took his last breath. In suburban Franklin, outside Detroit, he was surrounded by family members destined to share in his estimated fortune of three quarters of a billion dollars.

Column after column, page after page, day after day, both Detroit papers rained unrestrained adulation on Fisher's memory. The headlines said it all:

"Max Fisher: A Lifetime Of Power And Passion"

"Max Fisher Leaves the World a Better Place"

"With Grace, Dealmaker Did It All"

"GOP Valued His Financial Clout, Savvy"

"Max Fisher's Sense Of Duty Defined His Whole Existence"

"'He is everything to us,' Metro Detroit Jews say'"

"Friends, Family Gather To Lay To Rest A Giant"

Tributes poured in from across the nation and around the world, some of the most fervent coming from Republican presidents, present and past. But one important aspect of Max Fisher's extraordinary life seemed to get short shrift: his featured role as a top fund-raiser for and confidante to Richard Nixon. Only a few of the multitude of stories on Fisher and his legacy even mentioned Nixon. Of course, with coverage that was clearly determined to remain worthy of the heroic nature of its subject, this was not surprising.

More than three decades ago, in the final chapter of *JoAnn D'Ark and the Prince Of Detroit*, I had written about "powerful, arbitrary and deceitful men who did not hesitate to impose their personal values or to protect their own positions of wealth and influence by using the favor, the pay-off, the cover-up and the lie..."

According to the date attached to the book's foreword, I had written those words and completed the manuscript not quite a month before the Watergate break-in on June 17, 1972. Twenty-six months later Richard Nixon had resigned in disgrace and left office revealed to the world as a liar, a deceiver, a criminal and, with the release of those infamous White House tapes, as a virulent anti-Semite.

Transcripts of those thousands of hours of taped conversations are littered with Nixon's references to "Jew boys" and "kikes." Among the lowlights:

His unqualified agreement when the Reverend Billy Graham complains bitterly about the Jews' "stranglehold" on the media and blames them for "all the pornography."

His complaints that Washington "is full of Jews" and that "most Jews are disloyal."

To aide John Ehrlichman: "John, we have the power. Are we using it to investigate...the Jews—you know, that are stealing in every direction? Are we going after their tax returns? I can only hope that we're doing a little persecuting."

To chief of staff, H.R. Haldeman: "Generally speaking you can't trust the bastards. They turn on you. Am I wrong or right?" (Haldeman agreed.)

For decades rumors had circulated that Nixon was anti-Semitic, no doubt making more of a chore Fisher's fund-raising for him in the Jewish community. When the tapes were finally released by court order, many Jews expressed outrage, or at least dismay. Not Fisher. Still loyal even decades later, he was quoted as saying:

"I just felt, well, that's all part of history. Have you ever said things in private that you didn't want anybody to hear? That's the same thing that happened. I'm sure that every president has some nasty words to say or used some profane language."

I have no doubt Max rests in peace.

That's not a wish penned from an ironic or forgiving heart. Rather a cold statement of fact perceived through my own personal screen of notions, guesses and philosophical surmises. I'm of the view that Max exists now, like Hitler, Gandhi and the Sudanese child who starved to death a minute ago, only in the memories of others.

The remainder of my own memories of Max assembled over the past 30-plus years I'll set down here with economy. Actually, there were a number of experiences that, in a sense, re-connected Max to me in the years after *Murder* disappeared from bookstore shelves and ended up in my basement.

The first was a series of meetings that took place for more than a year in private homes in the northwest suburbs of Detroit. Small, more or less informal book clubs or reading circles were popular in those days in the Jewish community (they probably still are, but I've since lost touch), and I began to get invitations to attend these gatherings and to speak about my book.

The folks I met at these sessions were invariably gracious, kind and curious. Invariably, after a discussion of research methods, issues raised by the events described, and questions about what I personally thought of this or that person in the book, someone would frame a question that would go something like: "We've heard that something unfortunate happened to your book, and we wondered, would you be willing to talk about it?" And I would say, "Of course."

No one ever appeared to have a problem believing my story, and it was clear that word was being passed from club to club that the author would be more than happy to come to your next meeting free of charge and offer the inside dope on this scandal. Thus, the calls continued for quite awhile, every month or two, and, given the close-knit nature of the Jewish community, I had no doubt that Max Fisher, probably sooner than later, had been told exactly what I was saying about him in these private sessions around town. Yet I never heard a word of complaint from Max or from anyone else about what I was doing or saying.

Occasionally at these meetings, someone would ask where they could purchase my book. I would say, "Only from my basement." I soon learned to bring along a few copies in the car. And rather than try to give the copy away free, which was my first inclination, I also found it ultimately less awkward to say the price was a nominal $5.

This was essentially the only way I ever sold *Murder in the Synagogue*. In addition to my futile attempts to interest commercial and university presses in re-issuing the book, I even tried offering it to publishers in several European countries. That rather fanciful effort went nowhere as well. And after moves between three suburban Detroit homes over the past three decades, most of those original 1400 copies I secured from Prentice-Hall still reside in my current basement warehouse.

As for the book you hold in your hands, in the months both before and after I finished writing it, my strong suspicion was that if I could not even give away *Murder in the Synagogue* — as I was basically ready to do in order to see it back in print — there was precious little hope that *JoAnn D'Ark and The Prince Of Detroit* would ever see a publisher's imprint.

Of course that didn't stop me from pitching it to numerous literary agents, all of whom I had introductions to from people in the business. Most writers will recognize all too well the lines I received in response: "The list is very full." "This is not for me...good luck with it elsewhere." "I'm not sufficiently enthusiastic." "I couldn't give this the effort it deserves." In a number of cases there was no response at all.

I tried several book publishers directly. While I realized that the publication of my manuscript meant almost certain lawsuits by the publisher and a man of substantial power and influence with enormously deep pockets, I told myself with the drowning logic of a man swimming too far from shore, that I might find a gambler ready to pit the risk against the potentially lucrative notoriety of a major scandal.

This led me to the infamous Lyle Stuart, the so-called Bad Boy of American publishing, the author of a scandalous expose of Walter Winchell and the maverick publisher of such salacious titles as *The Anarchists Cookbook*. With a reputed relish for defying the powers that be, Stuart appeared to be the kind of player who, as I wrote in my letter to him, "might be interested in this story and would know what to do with it." Sent along with a copy of *Murder*, my letter laid out bluntly what Max Fisher had done to it and asked if Stuart would like to see the opening chapters of my book about the suppression. From a hospital bed in Jamaica where he was recovering from a broken thigh bone, Stuart wrote back to say he'd give my chapters a "careful, quick, and personal reading."

That would be, in fact, the only time an agent or publisher would ever agree to look at even part of *JoAnn D'Ark and The Prince Of Detroit*. Six weeks later Stuart wrote back: "I've given this a careful reading and I'm afraid it just isn't anything that captures my fancy enough for us to get involved with it. Sorry."

Stuart's rejection led me to re-think the economic realities of book publishing and thus to write the suppression story as a magazine piece. I tried the 6300-word article with a wide range of periodicals, from Rolling Stone to The New York Review of Books. While a number of editors responded with condolences, no one cared to join me on the risky limb I occupied.

The culmination of this effort came near the end of 1972, when I received a letter from an editor at The Atlantic Monthly. He wrote that the magazine had decided that my article was not "altogether successful at rising above its narrow purposes as a story of idiosyncratic tribulation."

So, according to the folks at The Atlantic, what happened to my book was simply an unfortunate special case. But within two years the publication of another Prentice-Hall book would prove that my tribulation was in fact not idiosyncratic.

In 1974, four years after *Murder in the Synagogue*'s brief appearance, Prentice-Hall published *Du Pont: Behind The Nylon Curtain* by Gerard Colby Zilg. I knew nothing about this book until the fall of 1981 when I read a story in the Washington Post about its author's lawsuit against Prentice-Hall and the Du Pont family. The Post story (9/22/81) had a New York dateline:

> A single telephone call from a Du Pont public relations man to the Book-of-the-Month Club financially doomed an unflattering history of the Du Pont family and its businesses, according to allegations made in a trial here yesterday.

> In a case with potentially broad implications for the publishing industry, the author of the history alleges that his 1974 book was irredeemably damaged because his publisher and a book club were intimidated by Du Pont interests.

Zilg, who subsequently simplified his pen name to Gerard Colby, charged breach of contract by Prentice-Hall and interference with contract relations by Du Pont. He sought $350,000 in compensatory damages and $1 million in punitive damages for lost royalties, paperback licensing and other types of book sales.

Colby established that a Prentice-Hall salesman, "under orders," had helped get the book's unedited manuscript into the hands of the

Du Pont family. Soon thereafter, officials at the Book-of-the-Month Club's Fortune Book Club received a call from Du Pont company officials who reported that their lawyers had found the book "scurrilous and actionable." The BOMC promptly cancelled its deal with Prentice-Hall. The publisher in turn quickly cut its first print run of 10,000 by a third, at which point, according to the company's own documents, the book could not price profitably "according to any conceivable formula." Prentice-Hall also slashed the advertising budget in half and scaled back promotional efforts to a few TV and radio appearances.

All of this had a familiar ring, but how had the author Colby learned about it? Unlike my experience, the book's editor defied company officials, who had sworn him to secrecy, and brought this inside information to Colby. Then, even more remarkably, a Prentice-Hall lawyer, its lead counsel, took the story to the New York Times. On January 21, 1975, two weeks after the Times had published a highly positive review of the book, the newspaper reported on the Du Ponts' effort to stop the book. Yet, in spite of good reviews and the Times report on the scandal, with insufficient copies available in stores during the all-important holiday season, the book died quickly.

As I've mentioned, I would not learn for another several years about the Du Pont book, what was done to it, and the outcome of the author's lawsuit. I'll get to all that shortly, but in the meantime let me pick up my own story again briefly.

With my divorce final, making some kind of a living had become a serious concern. Clearly I needed to put my frustration over *Murder in the Synagogue* behind me, and so it was at this point that I started giving away my remaining copies of the manuscript of *JoAnn D'Ark and the Prince Of Detroit*.

I concentrated on trying to interest editors at national magazines in what I thought were some of the region's best stories. With the auto companies heading for trouble and the post-riot city in sad financial straits, crime (rampant murder and drug dealing), corruption and various brands of sleaze were prime topics.

I pitched everything from the off-beat (a prison break that utilized a helicopter, an effort by the hotel and restaurant employees union to organize the town's topless dancers) to what seemed to me the city's most significant story in those early years of the decade: its devastating heroin trade. Detroit's creative new wrinkle on this urban plague was the employment of children to sell on the street. Because there were few if any legal consequences even if police caught them in the act, pre- and early-teens were now routinely involved. It seemed clear to me that what we were seeing was a new social order in the making, a new path, pattern, archetype and way of life for children growing up in the city. And not just those from the much analyzed underclass, but also from working and middle-class homes, kids who despite their advantages, were also lured by the excitement, instant gratification and entrepreneurial promise of peddling illicit narcotics, a business that was already spawning its own dress, lingo, music and code of ethics.

My pitches met with little or no success. Typically there would be a line or two of encouragement and then the kiss off. Subsequently I'd write the piece for a local magazine, which would make it a cover story and pay me a fraction of what a national publication would have offered. I told myself I needed an agent and that national editors weren't particularly interested in the plight of a sad-sack town like Detroit. If I really wanted to free-lance in a major way, I told myself, I needed to move to New York. But that wasn't really an option. With joint custody of our 9-year-old son, I knew I could never leave him behind.

What I really needed was a new book project. In 1974 I decided the city's drug trade had supplied one. The Pingree Street Conspiracy put several cops and several alleged drug dealers—a total of 16 altogether—on trial in one Detroit courtroom. The story seemed to have everything: juicy and frightening tales of corruption, murder and betrayal from inside the drug trade; a large cast of colorful, fascinating and disgusting characters, including a fearless, crusading internal affairs cop, corrupt police officers, murderers, drug dealers, pimps and assorted lowlifes; some of the best legal talent in the city; and, presiding over it all, Justin Ravitz, a brilliant young jurist nationally known as America's first Marxist judge.

For six months I covered this judicial extravaganza everyday basically on spec, although under a pseudonym I wrote a story every week that was published in a local tabloid. And then I finally found an agent willing to take me on along with my new book project.

At the end of 1974 I took the suggestion of my first editor at Prentice-Hall, Gladys Carr, and wrote to an agent with something of a legendary name in post-World War II American publishing. At one point or another over the previous three decades, the man had guided the careers of such luminaries as P.G. Wodehouse, Arthur C. Clark, Norman Mailer and Henry Miller. Frankly, given my experience with prospective agents over the previous few years, I had not invested my query with much hope. I had also not said a word about Max Fisher and the suppression of *Murder in the Synagogue*.

When the distinctive gray stationery arrived in the mail from the Scott Meredith Literary Agency, my eyes raced through its opening lines, and I was amazed to learn that Meredith had already read *Murder*, "and I admire it very much. We'll be very happy to act as your agents..." As for my new book project, he pronounced the material I had sent along on the Pingree Street Conspiracy to be "very good," and about the prospect of selling a book on the subject he wrote, "I'm very excited about it's possibilities."

Though in later years his agency would allow its reputation to be tainted somewhat by the frowned upon practice of charging desperately eager, would-be authors a fee for the agency's estimation of their manuscript's viability, Meredith's own reputation for intelligent taste and innovative marketing seemed to be exactly what I was looking for. As I would soon learn, his responses were invariably prompt, full of superlatives about the stories and articles I was sending him and loaded with cheerful optimism about any project he agreed to take on.

Within a few weeks, however, I wrote to him about a project he would not agree to take on. Even so, he did offer extensive advice on whether I should allow a local magazine called Detroit Discovery to publish my article on the suppression of *Murder in the Synagogue*. The magazine had featured a number of my stories over the previous several months but (in what I preferred to think was an unrelated development) was soon to go out of business. Its young Jewish publisher was peeved at the area's business community, because, he felt, it had failed to provide him with appropriate support. And so he had decided to run my piece, with notoriety explosive enough to either save his magazine or send it to oblivion with a considerable bang. He had already designed the issue's cover, with a photograph of a copy of *Murder* shot full of holes, the spent shells in the foreground, and the headline, "The Murder of a Book."

In my letter to Meredith dated January 27, 1975, I explained the situation. I mentioned that "my informant is nervous about the pressures that might be exerted to get her to change her story." I closed with this paragraph:

"I want you to know that I have great faith in your judgment and will carefully consider any advice you may offer. The publication of this story seemed very important in the past, but what is vital to me now is the chance to reach as many people as possible with as much good writing as I can produce. If the appearance of this story in Detroit Discovery would help, wonderful. If it would hurt, I'll tell [the editor] to forget it."

In response, Meredith's letter, dated February 4, 1975, opened with this:

"On the plus side, my feeling is that there's very little if anything to be gained by publishing the article."

Well, I thought, if that's on the plus side, my decision is already obvious. But of course I kept reading:

"Although you have some rather damaging admissions from Prentice-Hall personnel of a circumstantial nature, the real crux of your case rests entirely on the statement of a single person. And, quite apart from any consideration of whether she's telling the truth or not, this makes for a very weak case in the minds of most people."

Yes, once again the argument that having only one source made it problematic to proceed. Meredith introduced another dominant theme with these lines:

"But, even granting that there was collusion between Max Fisher and Prentice-Hall to suppress the book and even granting that people would be convinced of this by your article, regrettably the reaction to it would be one of virtually universal indifference."

The problem, said the agent, was that "one reads exactly this same kind of accusation with regard to some book or other on the average of every other month." Thus, this kind of charge was so commonplace that "the whole question just becomes immensely boring." A bit later he wrote: "The publication of the article will do your career no damage whatsoever, because of the indifference to such cases as cited above..."

For the same reason, Meredith even minimized the possibility of legal retaliation: "There is, as you know, some small chance that Max Fisher will institute a lawsuit against you."

Some small chance? There'd be so little interest in the charge that Fisher had squelched my book that he wouldn't even bother to sue? That certainly seemed questionable. But why all this talk from Meredith on how accusations about the suppression of books by American publishers were so commonplace?

Perhaps because just one week before I had written to him about Prentice-Hall's suppression of *Murder in the Synagogue*, the New York Times had published its expose of Prentice-Hall's similar treatment of *Du Pont: Behind the Nylon Curtain*. Well-respected reporter Alden Whitman's piece appeared in the Times on January 21, 1975. I wrote to Meredith asking for his advice on January 27, and he wrote back on February 4. And yet Meredith said not a word about an article that would certainly have caught his attention in a major way, given his role as a big-time literary agent.

At that moment, knowing that another Prentice-Hall author had suffered a fate similar to mine at the hands of our publisher, and that a story exposing the details had just appeared in the New York Times, I would most likely have brought my information to Whitman at the Times and offered to join forces with Gerard Colby. Perhaps nothing would have come of doing those things, but we'll never know, because Scott Meredith's letter made no mention of the Times' piece.

At another point in his letter to me, Meredith wrote: "...Prentice-Hall have, in fact, done nothing whatever illegal. Neither they, nor any other publisher, are contractually obligated to publish a book for which they've contract [*sic*] responsibly."

But that was exactly the major point at issue six years later in the legal action that Gerard Colby brought against Prentice-Hall and the Du Ponts over their suppression of his book. The trial judge found that Prentice-Hall had in fact failed to perform basic obligations, such as promoting, advertising and distributing the Du Pont book and thus was liable for breach of contract. Colby was awarded $24,250 to compensate for lost royalties.

The Du Ponts fared much better at the hands of the judge. Ignoring the Du Pont company's unfounded threats of legal action, while using terms such as "actionable" and "scurrilous," all of which was carefully documented at trial, the judge decided that the Du Ponts were simply exercising their freedom of speech and expressing their opinion of the book.

Two years later a three-judge federal appeals panel in New York reversed the decision against Prentice-Hall. It did so not by finding any error of fact or law. Rather it gave the book a whole new reading. The book was, said the panel, a "Marxist view of history" that would have only limited potential readership. Ignoring expert testimony and the publisher's own sales records, the panel thus found that Prentice-Hall had good reason to kill the book.

What's my judgment today about Scott Meredith's advice? Certainly it was a skillful effort to discourage me (without seeming to try) from going public, delivered by a major player in business with the publishing establishment. If, in fact, he decided not to alert me to the Times story about the suppression of another Prentice-Hall book, it was just one more small betrayal. But then I was clearly anxious to let Meredith's agency perform its magic for my career, and I was hesitant to say or do anything that might jeopardize our connection. Soon after I received his response, I recalled my article from Detroit Discovery.

Over the next year and a half my dealings with Meredith and his agency would alternate between hopeful promise and frustrating disappointment. Often he or one of his junior agents would respond to one of my stories or articles or project ideas with praise and enthusiasm. "This is very good. We'll take it right out" became a mantra. But almost invariably the agency's efforts to sell the piece for me would bear no fruit. Even my new book project, with which I intended to document the urban nightmare of illicit narcotics, and about which Meredith had seemed so confident, ultimately went nowhere. He reported that the last publishing house editor he approached had told him, "This is a black book," (meaning its appeal would be primarily to African Americans) "and blacks don't buy books."

This seemed both racist and wrongheaded, and it dumped me right back where I had been, laboring in the provinces, unable to sell my work, even with one of New York's top literary agencies hawking it.

Finally, I moved in a different direction. Free lance work with the state arm of the National Endowment for the Humanities led to my creating TV documentaries, which is the way I would make a living for much of the next three decades.

Twice doing this kind of work, I crossed paths, so to speak, with

Max Fisher. First, in the early '80s I was assigned to write and produce a half-hour special on Fisher and Henry Ford II as the two most powerful men in Detroit. The TV station executives who gave me the assignment did not know about my history with Fisher, and I simply went about my business, taking footage that had already been shot for a news series and shaping it into a 30-minute documentary. Naturally, the result lauded Fisher and Ford for their extraordinary contributions to the community and seemed to please everyone — except the writer/producer.

Ten years later I drew a different kind of assignment: creating from scratch a half-hour documentary on Fisher's step-daughter Mary, who had recently announced that she was HIV positive. I worked closely with Mary, directing shoots both in Detroit and at her home in Florida. I interviewed her a number of times, met her two children, wrote the script and oversaw the edit.

I ended up liking Mary Fisher. I found her bright, attractive and brave, a talented artist and admirably committed to spreading an important message. As she told the Republican National Convention in the summer of '92: "HIV only asks one thing of those it attacks: Are you human?" In all of my contacts with her, including a lot of casual, off-the-record conversation, I never picked up the slightest indication that she was aware of her father's impact on my book and my life. And because it seemed like the professional thing to do, I said nothing about *Murder in the Synagogue*.

At one point late in the process I needed to confirm some information with Mary and called the number she had given me to reach her at home with her parents in Franklin.

Max Fisher answered.

Of course I had thought of the possibility when I dialed the number and wondered what an exchange might be like. Now that he was actually on the line, I felt strangely calm as I asked for Mary.

She wasn't in. Was there a message for her?

Yes, I said, "Would you ask her to call Tom LoCicero." I spelled my last name.

There was a pause. Was this 83-year-old man at the other end of the line trying to place the name? Did the name and its significance register immediately?

There was something about the quality of that silence or about the way he finally said, "Okay," that suggested the latter.

I said I was producing a TV special on Mary.

"Oh," he said, "I'll give her the message."

I said thank you and goodbye. And I hung up the phone.

That was it, the only time I ever spoke directly with Max Fisher, and I said absolutely nothing at all about that old matter between us.

Why? Because, as with Mary, I thought it was the professional thing to do? Because I generally avoided confrontation? Because after all those years, two decades, in fact, what difference would it make? Because if I really wanted to speak to this man about what he had done, why would I choose to do it now, when I was in the process of telling the important story of his step-daughter's battle with AIDS?

Maybe all of the above.

When I re-connected with my old professor friend Leo McNamara and we began lunching together on a regular basis—when I re-acquired from Leo the manuscript of my "lost book," as I began calling it—and especially several months later, when I actually began reading my old manuscript for the first time in more than 30 years, I began to think about what it might be like to meet again with Avren Strager. That's the real name of the woman who came to me more than 35 years ago with the shocking news that she had heard Max Fisher say he had arranged with my publisher to "squelch" my book, the woman whose identity I had tried to protect by re-naming her JoAnn D'Ark.

She had on many occasions pledged her willingness to "go public" about what she heard Max Fisher say about *Murder in the Synagogue*. If needed to insure justice for *Murder*, she would put her name and reputation on the line. Yes, I had found her unequivocally vouched for by the likes of Rabbi Adler's widow Goldie and by Rabbi Max Kapustin at the Wayne State University Hillel Center. But even if those respected community figures decided to openly support her, going public certainly promised to be a distinctly unpleasant experience. At her temple, she had already learned what it would feel like to be ostracized by life-long friends and acquaintances, and she had been shaken.

Although several other people had been in the room to hear Fisher say what she reported hearing from him, no one was willing to come forward with her. It was clear that her own father and husband were part of this group, but while her husband Melvin Strager had privately endorsed his wife's reliability, she was always adamant that neither of them should be asked to publicly support what she was saying. They both had business concerns, her husband Mel as an engineer with his own firm and her father, Sidney Foreman, as an accountant who had done deals over the years with Max Fisher. They both had families to support. They should not be asked to share in her act of conscience.

And so in writing about the suppression of *Murder in the Synagogue* in a book that admittedly had a very slim chance of being published, my arrangement with Avren Strager was that I would use a pseudonym for her, unless and until someone was ready to make the story public. At the time of my exchange with Scott Meredith on the advisability of giving the story to Detroit Discovery, I had not even spoken with Avren about the possibility. Only if my decision were to let the magazine publish the story, would I break the news of what was coming.

As I began to move away from the frustrating experience of trying to do something about the suppression of my book and to concentrate instead on new stories and, finally, a new career, I spoke with Avren less and less often, until we ultimately just lost touch. It was simply better for both of us, it seemed, if each of us went our separate ways. I was in that mindset, described earlier, of relentlessly moving forward while discarding and forgetting the past. And so for close to 30 years I thought about Avren Strager only rarely.

Then as I re-read the manuscript Leo had saved, the reality of this extraordinary woman came rushing back at me: her pluck and courage, her sharp intelligence, blunt opinion, business savvy and cultural naiveté, her firm conscience and commitment to principle, her devotion to her people and her religion, her prickly, sometimes difficult moods, the narrow insularity of her life and finally her remarkable decision to break the boundaries and come to me.

What would it be like to see and talk to her again and, after such an intense experience shared so long ago, to compare notes on three decades of life lived with no contact or knowledge of each other? Our meeting would certainly be the culmination of the epilogue I was already planning in my head to serve as the closing part of the frame for the manuscript I was finally holding in my hands once again.

So how would I find her? Well, of course, I would start with that remarkable tool not even dreamed of back in those days when Avren and I were chatting often on the phone, but which I now used so often. I would google her. Then if nothing useful turned up, I'd focus on the Detroit Jewish News, where a wedding anniversary, a child's graduation or marriage, an aunt's or a father's passing might be recorded with a reference or affiliation that might prove helpful.

And so I casually clicked on Google Search near the top of my computer screen and typed in Avren Strager. Within 0.34 seconds I was given three results. At the top I was asked "Did you mean Avren *Stranger?*" Nope. I looked at the first results:

"Campaign contributors to Chrysler, Richard R.: Strager, Avren, Strager, Melvin..."

Chrysler, I knew, was a former Republican businessman who had served in Congress back in the '90s from Michigan's 8th district. So Avren and her husband had contributed to one of Chrysler's campaigns.

The second result was a variation of the first with contributions listed by zip code. So now I knew their zip back in the '90s. The third result said:

"Death Notices 5/01: Strager, Melvin, Beloved husband of Lori Strager and the late Avren Strager."

I was stunned. Foolishly I had not even thought about the possibility that Avren Strager was no longer alive. In addition to the news that he had re-married, Melvin's obit said he had left a son, three daughters and three grandchildren. When I first met them, Avren was 30, and she and Mel had two children under the age of four. On one of the people-search sites I learned that Avren Strager had been born in 1941 and died in 1994 at the age of 52. My heart felt crushed. She had been taken at a time when most of us have just begun to see our children forging careers and marriages of their own and perhaps giving us the sweet pleasures of grandchildren.

There'd be no reunion now, no comparing of notes about the last three decades. I had waited too long, and Avren had not even survived two decades. Her death at 52 felt like a reprimand now, an indictment of the way I had lived, until only recently devoted to compartmentalizing my life and closing myself off from my past and from the people who had been important to me back then. Finally, I recalled Avren talking about one of the reasons she felt so close to Rabbi Adler: he had helped her through two bouts of an often-fatal illness as a child. Perhaps that illness—she hadn't offered, and I hadn't asked, but my guess back then was leukemia—had returned a third time to finish its grim resolve.

I thought of Max Fisher still enjoying the comforts of his home and family at the age of 96. The fates had given him almost twice as many years as they had granted to Avren Strager.

* * *

Over the past few years I've thought about trying this up-dated version of my "lost book" with the traditional world of publishing. Maybe there'd be a chance now with a diminished prospect of lawsuits (Prentice-Hall's trade division was disbanded twenty years ago and its education division sold a couple of times since, most recently to Pearson Education, Inc.). But would anyone be interested in this 40-year-old story?

Finally, I queried three publishers and two-dozen agents. Most did not respond at all. A handful sent standard rejections. But one university press editor and one agent (a fellow who also publishes his own guide to the business, with lists of houses and agents) asked to look at the book. I sensed more curiosity than interest, but of course I sent it along. The agent responded with an impersonal rejection; the editor said the book did not fit with the future direction of the press.

But it was about this time that I began to realize the world had changed. Specifically, the publishing business was being turned on its ear. Digital publishing had exploded in the face of the traditional houses, and on the Web writers and readers were using new ways to find each other. Published authors, and those who wanted to be, were putting up websites to showcase their books, distributing them through the new digital sellers like Amazon and Barnes&Noble, and promoting them with the social media that not long ago had seemed to me a waste of time.

So belatedly I joined the revolution. I read everything I could find on this new world of digital publishing and regularly visited blogs that did a good job of explaining, dissecting and promoting the revolution. The plan was to put up a website and sell my books, *Squelched* and *Murder* first, then others I'd spent lots of time on in recent years.

One day on a visit to one of my favorite blogs, I noticed a short quote on how a writer should never wait until the next book to use something good he's come up with. Just toss it into the current book.

The message seemed neither well-crafted nor particularly wise, but the name of its author was a revelation: Tam Mossman.

A quick google search established that this was the same Tam Mossman who had worked as an editor at Prentice-Hall, the young guy, maybe five years my junior, who had worked on *Murder*, and from whom I had never heard after I confronted the publisher on its collusion with Max Fisher. Over four decades I had never seen a reference to Tam Mossman, and now I learned why. He had continued working for several years at Prentice-Hall where his claim to fame was editing all the controversial "Seth" books by author Jane Roberts. A channeling superstar, Roberts served as a conduit for someone named Seth, who resided somewhere in the afterlife. Both in her books and in public appearances, she channeled Seth's otherworldly news and wisdom.

Then in 1975 Mossman discovered that he too had the ability to channel. He performed at the University of Virginia in Charlottesville, the first of many public demonstrations offering "material" from his own spirit guy named "James." Later Mossman left publishing to start a channeling journal called Metapsychology, described by one expert as, in its day, "the premier journal of its kind in the world." James often spoke through Mossman in its pages.

Now admittedly, I have never had much patience with spiritualist doings, and back in those days I had decided channeling was just more New Age nonsense. So Mossman and I had obviously traveled very different paths. Was he still channeling? Hard to tell, since his google trail had gone rather cold. But recently he had published a book called *7.625 Strategies in Every Best-Seller*. So he was back to books, though he had no author's website and no contact info on his publisher's site. I finally found an email address and wrote him a long note that began:

> Hey Tam,
>
> It's been a while. About 40 years. Hope you're doing well. Just wanted to let you know that I'm soon to publish a book I'm sure will be of special interest to you.

I followed with the lengthy description of *Squelched* that was part of my pitch to the agents, laying out the book's strange history and including the fact that in the mid-'70s Prentice-Hall had also suppressed another of its books, *Du Pont: Behind the Nylon Curtain*. I finished with this:

> Of course, you're mentioned many times in *Squelched*, but I was fair, I think, even kind to you, although I made clear that you must have known full-well what Prentice-Hall was doing to *Murder*.

> ...I thought why not offer you a chance to emulate your former fellow editor and the company attorney (both remarkable guys) who went to the author and to the NY Times with the story of what Prentice Hall was doing to the Du Pont book. They did the right thing, and so could you. Even if belated, it would be good for the soul.

Okay, so that last line was a bit snarky, but I fully expected at most a simple denial that he was aware of any untoward machinations with *Murder* by Prentice-Hall. A few hours later this response arrived:

> Tom, I'm not sure what you hope I can do with your "pitch." Yes, I have successfully agented books for two authors whose work I believed in. But I'm not affiliated with any publisher—and am working on projects of my own that leave me no time for per-hour editorial assistance, aside from the suggestion that authors read *7.625 Strategies in Every Best-Seller*, available from BookLocker. Because I do not consider myself a public figure and intend to keep it that way, I do *not* want my name to appear in any book. In the past, such mentions have only brought me unwanted queries.

> Other authors whose books I contracted—and which are still in print—have respected that and cited me as simply "my editor." Now that you understand my desire for privacy, I trust you'll follow their lead.

Best,

Tam

Was he senile? By my guess he'd be in his mid-60s, so not likely. I had clearly requested information on what he saw going on at Prentice-Hall 40 years ago, and he thinks I want his editing help? He's just published a book but insists he's not a public figure and doesn't want his name used in mine? I wrote back with two sentences:

> Thanks, Tam, for your prompt response. I'll give
> your request for anonymity due consideration.

Less than two hours later I got a new, very different message. Here's the whole thing:

> You should remember that I was not the editor
> who contracted *Murder*, simply the one assigned
> to edit it for Gladys Carr. Production asked me
> to trim your manuscript because it was too long
> to price out effectively — and had vastly too
> much pointless, irrelevant minutiae. The only
> pressure I felt was to get the book down to
> manageable size.
>
> Several titles I later contracted myself
> were acceptable to me, but the house declined to
> publish them because of conflicts of interest
> with corporate policy or unforeseen sudden
> competition. Authors kept their advances, and
> were free to publish elsewhere.
>
> That's how it works in the real world. NO
> publisher is going to "suppress" a title by first
> publishing it for anyone to see and then failing
> to promote it! That would not only waste $$$
> but defeat the purpose.
>
> Any book can get a good review from *someone*.
> But I recall a salesman asking me (rhetorically),
> "Why are we publishing this book? It's boring!"
> And salesmen tend to skim over a book they feel

won't sell.

I also note that though *Murder* is still listed on Amazon, it has picked up no reviews at all. That puts it in the same no-opinion boat as Kitty Dukakis' *Now You Know.* At P-H, we used to call these titles "News Story" books, which go on remainder as soon as the media buzz dies down. And after *Murder*, we quit contracting them.

Even so, a salesworthy book could be compiled documenting cases of covert censorship in the publishing industry — as long as it used plenty of examples to back up its claim and managed to fault the editorial elitism that has spawned so many successful independent houses.

But a book alleging ONE 40-year-old "conspiracy" — that only victimized one single author! — is going to be passed over as a woe-is-me wheeze. Especially if it makes the naive claim that a house sought to suppress a book by offering it for sale!

I assume you intend to self-publish, but be aware that writing about someone's motives /actions without asking for his comments is permissible, *if* you can't locate the individual and say so in a disclaimer.

But if you can — and if he disputes the facts, and you ignore his objections and go ahead with your version anyway — then attorneys will start earning their keep by asking what kind of "due consideration" you gave.

Though a bit more to the point, another strange response. Despite the nasty, aggressive, disparaging tone, the closest he comes to an answer is the statement: *"The only pressure I felt was to get the book down to manageable size."* And the assertion: *"NO publisher is going to 'suppress' a title by first publishing it for anyone to see and then failing to promote it! That would not only waste $$$ but defeat the purpose."*

On the first point, the only pressure I ever thought Tam Mossman was under back then was to do his job and keep his head down. And he wasn't even tasked with trimming the manuscript. I did that myself after rejecting the hack job done by those 6 or 7 other editors Mossman himself had told me about.

As for his assertion that no publisher would ever do such a thing, he seems to contradict himself a few lines later: "*Even so, a salesworthy book could be compiled documenting cases of covert censorship in the publishing industry as long as it used plenty of examples to back up its claim...*"

I thought back to my meeting with Gladys Carr in New York after I learned what had been done to *Murder*. Yes, such things occasionally happened, she had said back then, but the only person at Prentice-Hall who would have made the decision to squelch was the trade division president, Wilbur Eastman.

Of course, Tam Mossman had not been responsible for what happened to *Murder*. And only he can say what he could or should have told me at the time. The editor who brought the inside story to Gerard Colby about his book on the Du Ponts was thereafter fired.

Actually, according to Colby and others, this kind of secret suppression was common enough that in the '70s industry insiders had a term for it: "privishing." A book would be "privished," or privately published as opposed to truly published.

In "The Price of Liberty," one of several essays about suppression in the media collected in a book entitled *Into the Buzzsaw*, Colby wrote:

> The mechanism used is simple: cut off the book's life-support system by reducing the initial print run so that the book "cannot price profitably according to any conceivable formula," refuse to do reprints, drastically slash the book's advertising budget, and all but cancel the promotional tour. The publisher's purpose is to kill off a book that, for one reason or another, is considered "troublesome" or potentially so. This widespread activity must be done secretly because it constitutes a breach of contract, which, if revealed, could subject the publisher to legal liability.

Yes, that pretty much describes *Murder*'s plight.

So what about Mossman's unpleasant assessment of the sales potential of *Squelched*?

"*...a book alleging ONE 40-year-old "conspiracy" – that only victimized one single author! – is going to be passed over as a woe-is-me wheeze.*"

Not quite as elegant as the line from that Atlantic Monthly editor who called my story an "idiosyncratic tribulation" four decades ago.

But that's the beauty of our extraordinary new world of publishing. You don't really have to give a fig for what the old gatekeepers might think. Just toss your book into that amazing sea of digital interconnection now covering our globe, and see if it sinks or swims.

###

From T.V. LoCicero:

Word-of-mouth

It's vital to any author. If you enjoyed this book, please consider leaving a review at Amazon. It may be only a line or two, but it could make a big difference and would be deeply appreciated.

Be the First to Learn of a New Release

If you'd like to receive an auto email when the next book is released, please sign up at: http://eepurl.com/z26Vv

Your email address will never be shared, and you can unsubscribe at any time.

Say Hello

My website (http//www.tvlocicero) offers info, thoughts, photos, videos and much more. I'd love it if you come by and say hello. You can also get in touch on Facebook, or send me an email: tvloc1@netscape.net

www.ingramcontent.com/pod-product-compliance
Lightning Source LLC
Chambersburg PA
CBHW051724040426
42447CB00008B/957